CHALLENGE OF THE
WEST

A Canadian Retrospective from 1815–1914

CHALLENGE OF THE
WEST

A Canadian Retrospective from 1815–1914

J. Bradley Cruxton
W. Douglas Wilson

Toronto
Oxford University Press
1997

Oxford University Press Canada
70 Wynford Drive, Don Mills, Ontario M3C 1J9

Oxford   New York
Athens   Auckland   Bangkok   Calcutta
Cape Town   Chennai   Dar es Salaam   Delhi
Florence   Hong Kong   Istanbul   Karachi
Kuala Lumpur   Madrid   Melbourne
Mexico City   Mumbai   Nairobi   Paris
Singapore   Taipei   Tokyo   Toronto

and associated companies in
Berlin   Ibadan

OXFORD is a trademark of Oxford University Press

CANADIAN CATALOGUING IN PUBLICATION DATA

Cruxton, J. Bradley
    Challenge of the West: a Canadian retrospective from
1815–1914

Includes index.
ISBN 0-19-541286-9

1. Canada, Western—History.   I. Wilson, W. Douglas.
II. Title.

FC3206.C78 1997   971.2   C97-930011-8
F1060.C78 1997

Cover Design: Brett Miller
Text Design: Heather Delfino/Brett Miller/Linda Mackey

Cover photo: "The SS Beaver off Fort Victoria, 1846." Painting by
Adam Sherriff Scott. Hudson Bay Company Archives/Provincial
Archives of Manitoba/T8233

Printed in Canada

This book is printed on permanent (acid-free) paper.

1   2   3   4   5   01   00   99   98   97

CONTENTS

Acknowledgements

The authors wish to thank the editorial and production staff at Oxford University Press (Canada) who have worked with us on this book. In particular, we would like to thank our editor, Loralee Case; Susan Froud, Managing Director; Marian Marsh, Western Manager; Micaela Gates, Editorial Assistant; Joanna Gertler, Production Director; and Brett Miller, Designer for their creative advice, encouragement, and constant support.

Introduction

Have you ever stopped to think about how things are always changing? Try making a list of all that has changed in your life over the past year. Perhaps you have started a new school, moved to a new neighbourhood, or developed a new hobby. How have you changed as a result? And what about all the things that have changed around you? How have fashions, music, governments, and technology changed in the past year?

What does *change* really mean? It is to make or become different. What are the ways in which change can come about? Sometimes change just happens. Other times, we make a change happen. When we set out to make change, it can involve conflict or struggle.

Are there things you would like to change in your school? Perhaps you think the dress code or the length of your lunch break should be changed. List four or five things you would like to see changed at your school. Consider how you would bring about these changes. Might some of the changes lead to conflict? Would everyone agree to them? Do you feel strongly enough about a change to fight for it? If so, how would you fight for it? What effects might your method of fighting have?

Now, what changes would you suggest for Canada? How could you bring about these changes? Would you use the same process you would use to bring about change in your school? Write down some strategies for making changes happen in Canada. Do you think it is justified to use force to bring about change? Under what conditions?

There have been times in Canadian history when people believed that armed rebellion was the only way to make change happen. At these times some citizens were prepared to take up weapons against the government. You will learn about four rebellions in this book: the Rebellion of Upper Canada in 1837, the Rebellion of Lower Canada in 1837, the Red River Rebellion in 1869-1870, and the North-West Rebellion in 1885.

As you read about the ways in which change came to Canada, consider the following questions:

1. Why were some people angry with the government?
2. Who were the leaders on both sides? What groups of people supported them?
3. Were any peaceful solutions tried first?
4. Why did some people think armed rebellion was the only way to bring about change?
5. How did the rebels attempt to overthrow the government? When and where did this happen?
6. Why did each rebellion fail or succeed?
7. What major changes resulted for ordinary Canadians that affected the future development of Canada?

CHAPTER 1

Rebellion and Change in Upper and Lower Canada

THE BATTLE OF TORONTO

Monday night, 4 December 1837

All night long the church bells of Toronto sounded the alarm. People were in a panic. Just a few kilometres north of the capital, William Lyon Mackenzie was gathering a small army of rebels at Montgomery's Tavern. Armed with muskets, rifles, pitchforks, and clubs, the rebels were determined to seize the Parliament Buildings and take the governor prisoner. They would force him to give the people more influence in government.

Just before midnight, the sound of horses' hoofs was heard along Yonge Street. Citizens hurried out as an elected official, John Powell, breathlessly told his news. He described how he was stopped on Yonge Street, about 3 km beyond the city limits, by Mackenzie and a number of armed rebels. Shots had been fired, but Powell managed to escape and flee into Toronto in the dark.

The escape of Mr. John Powell

About the same time, more bad news reached the city. Colonel Moodie was a retired army officer who lived north of Montgomery's Tavern. All day he watched with alarm as rebel troops gathered at the tavern. He was determined to get this information to the governor. He set out by horse down Yonge Street but found the road blocked by the rebels. When Colonel Moodie tried to charge through the barricade, he was shot and left to die. One of Moodie's companions escaped and brought the news to the city.

The death of Colonel Moodie

Tuesday, 5 December 1837

Alarm grew in the city. Only 300 trained fighters were available to defend Toronto. Most troops had been sent to Lower Canada to put down the trouble there. Rumours spread quickly that the rebel force now numbered 5000. The governor of Upper Canada, Sir Francis Bond Head, placed his own family on a steamer in the Toronto harbour for safety.

That night 700 rebels hiked south on Yonge Street in the pitch dark. Some were armed with rifles but others carried nothing more than sharpened sticks, clubs, and pitchforks.

Near where Maple Leaf Gardens now stands, Sheriff Jarvis and twenty-seven troops ambushed the rebels. There was a great flash and roar as muskets went off. Both sides panicked. Mackenzie's force turned and retreated to Montgomery's Tavern. Sheriff Jarvis's force fled into the city. One member of the rebel force lay dead on the road.

Wednesday, 6 December 1837

Reinforcements began to arrive in Toronto by steamer from Hamilton and Scarborough. The main buildings of Toronto—the City Hall, the House of Parliament, the Bank of Upper Canada, and many private houses—were barricaded with thick planks. Stores closed, and meat and bread were scarce.

About 6 km west of Toronto, Mackenzie and Samuel Lount held up the stage coach carrying the mail on Dundas Street. They seized money and letters that contained vital information about the defence of the city. Two men, wounded in Tuesday night's battle, died from loss of blood.

Thursday, 7 December 1837

Anthony Van Egmond, an experienced soldier, arrived at Montgomery's Tavern and took control of the rebel forces. He was upset to find that he had only about 500 poorly equipped troops. Hundreds of Mackenzie's supporters from the outlying districts had not yet arrived.

At noon, Governor Head and about 600 loyalist troops marched north on Yonge Street to fight the rebels. Two smaller groups of troops moved north through woods and ploughed fields to the west and east of Yonge Street. The three companies planned to attack the rebel headquarters at Montgomery's Tavern.

At one o'clock, rebel scouts sent word to Mackenzie that the government forces were on the way. Van Egmond and about 200 armed rebels took up position in the woods on both sides of the street. The unarmed rebels remained behind at the tavern.

When the rebels opened fire, loyalist troops set up their two cannons and aimed into the woods. The loyalists, advancing through the woods, closed in behind the rebels. The rebels dropped their rifles and ran. Then the cannons were moved up and fired directly at the front of Montgomery's Tavern. The rebels inside poured out like bees from a hive and headed into the surrounding woods.

Governor Head ordered a thorough search of the tavern. Soldiers found a list of the names of all rebel supporters. Then the tavern was burned to the ground.

The fighting lasted less than half an hour. One rebel died immediately and eleven others were wounded, four of them dying afterwards. Five loyalists were wounded, none of them seriously. The rebellion was crushed. Mackenzie and other rebel leaders rode off swiftly to the north to avoid being taken prisoners. A reward of £1000 was issued for the capture and return of the rebel leader, William Lyon Mackenzie.

BATTLE OF MONTGOMERY'S FARM.

The battle at Montgomery's Tavern

WANTED

William Lyon Mackenzie

One Thousand Pounds,

to any one who will apprehend, and deliver up to Justice, WILLIAM LYON MACKENZIE: and FIVE HUNDRED POUNDS to any one who will apprehend, and deliver up to Justice, DAVID GIBSON – or SAMUEL LOUNT – or JESSE LLOYD – or SILAS FLETCHER – and the same reward and a free pardon will be given to any of their accomplices who will render this public service, except he or they shall have committed, in his own person, the crime of Murder or Arson.

And all, but the Leaders above-named, who have been seduced to join in this unnatural Rebellion, are hereby called to return to their duty to their Sovereign – to obey the Laws – and to live henceforward as good and faithful Subjects – and they will find the Government of the Queen as indulgent as it is just.

GOD SAVE THE QUEEN

Thursday, 3 o'clock, P.M.
7th Dec., 1837

☞ The Party of Rebels, under their Chief Leaders, is wholly dispersed, and flying before the Loyal Militia. The only thing that remains to be done, is to find them, and arrest them.

William Lyon Mackenzie wanted poster

Trouble in Upper Canada

A **rebellion** is an armed uprising against the government. In some cases, the leaders of the rebellion try to establish a new and independent organization in place of the existing government.

For a few days in December 1837, rebellion raged in Upper Canada. Toronto, the capital city with a population of about 12 000, was under attack by between 500 and 1000 armed colonists. The rebels marched on the city to overthrow the government and bring about changes they considered important. Why

would formerly law-abiding citizens take such a desperate step? And why did the rebellion fail?

Causes of Discontent

1. The Way the Colony Was Governed

In 1825, British North America was made up of six colonies and two territories. Each colony had an **Assembly** of elected colonists. The colony was divided into voting districts, and each district could elect representatives to the Assembly. The Assembly meetings made plans for the colony which, when written down, were

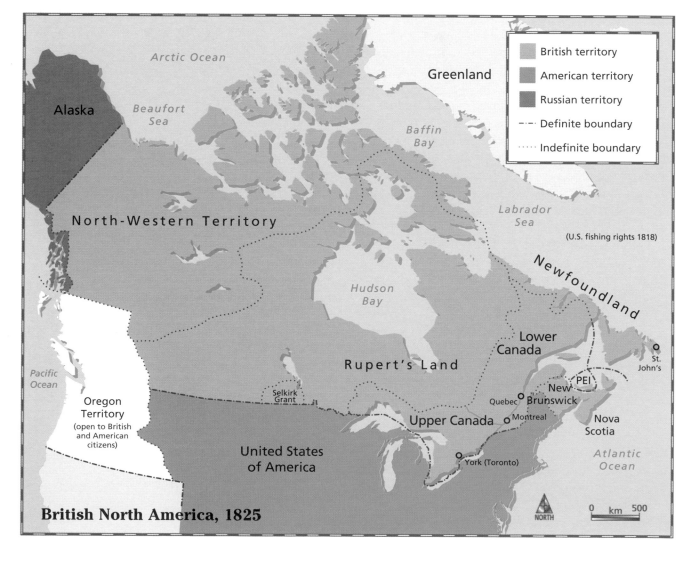

British North America, 1825

called **bills**. However, before a bill could become a law, it had to be approved by the governor and the councils.

Each colony had **executive** and **legislative councils** whose members were appointed by the governor. Often the governor and the small group of people he chose to advise him did not approve of the Assembly's bills. When this happened, they simply tossed the bills aside and ignored the wishes of the Assembly. So the people that the colonists elected to the Assembly only *helped* to make laws. The real power was in the hands of the governor and the councils. And because the councils were chosen, not elected, they did not have to worry about carrying out the wishes of the people.

Today, the Governor-General still must approve all laws passed by the Parliament of Canada. But those who advise the Governor-General are chosen from among the peoples' elected representatives in Parliament. The Governor-General must listen to the advice of these elected members. Thus she or he is *responsible* to the wishes of these members, and through them to the people of Canada who have elected them.

2. The Rulers of the Colony

The **governor** headed the government in the colonies. The governor, who in those days was always a man, was sent out from Britain as the personal representative of the reigning monarch. He was responsible to no one but the king or queen for his actions.

Usually the governor stayed for only a short time in North America. He was totally unfamiliar with the people and the way of life in the colony. Therefore, he depended a great deal on the advice of his executive and legislative councillors. The problem was that these councillors were always chosen from among the wealthy and influential people of the colony—judges, clergy, bankers, lawyers, military officers, and leading business people. A few were British, but most were **United Empire Loyalists** who had lived in the colony for many years. The United Empire Loyalists were originally Americans who had settled in British North America because they opposed the American Revolution against Britain. They remained loyal to the British crown. In most cases, they were close friends or related to one another. The colonists nicknamed this small group of Loyalists the **Family Compact**. They did not all come from the same family, but they all belonged to the highest social class. They believed that because they were wealthy and better educated, they could govern the colony much more effectively than other people.

The governor had the right to appoint all officials. He selected judges, sheriffs, justices of the peace, customs and immigration officers, postal officials, and Indian affairs officials. As head of the military forces, he appointed 1500 officers. He could give land grants and spend crown money for pensions to reward faithful supporters. Obviously, the British governors relied heavily on the advice of the Family Compact when naming people to these positions. It was said that one could not obtain a government job unless one was a member of the Family Compact. The farmers and their families were not included among these privileged few.

Some members of the Family Compact were capable and clever individuals. One of the most powerful was John Strachan, who later became the Anglican bishop of Toronto. He insisted that the Anglican Church should have special privileges and position in the colony. For example, until 1831 only Anglican clergy were licensed to perform marriages, even though the majority of the colonists belonged to other churches. Strachan was also interested in education. He founded Upper Canada College, a school for Anglican boys. In

3. The Problem of Land

Another source of discontent among the people of Upper Canada was the unfair way that land was granted to settlers. Much of this land had once been the home of aboriginal peoples. In 1836, Sir Francis Bond Head had convinced some of these aboriginal peoples to move to reservations in the Georgian Bay area. The best of their land was then given to members of the Family Compact or to their friends and favourites. For example, a former officer, Colonel Thomas Talbot, received a land grant of thousands of hectares along the north shore of Lake Erie. He had an arrangement with the government by which he got another 50 ha every time he sold 20 ha to a settler! Eventually, executive and legislative councillors and their families controlled 75 000 ha of land in Upper Canada.

The result was that less than 10 per cent of land in the colony was producing crops. Most of the best farmland was in the hands of people who had neither the skills for farming nor the desire to do so. They were simply waiting for the land to go up in value so they could sell it at a profit.

Farmers also objected to the government practice of granting one-seventh of all surveyed land to the Anglican Church. Other churches, such as the Presbyterians, Methodists, Baptists, and Roman Catholics, were not given equal grants. These huge tracts were known as **clergy reserves**. Colonists objected because church lands were often left uncleared and undeveloped while new settlers had to be content with poorer land. Large uncleared clergy reserves held up settlement because no roads were built through them. The dense woods harboured wolves, which attacked the settlers' livestock, and weeds, which contaminated their crops. It is little wonder that so many farmers joined the ranks of William Lyon Mackenzie's rebellion!

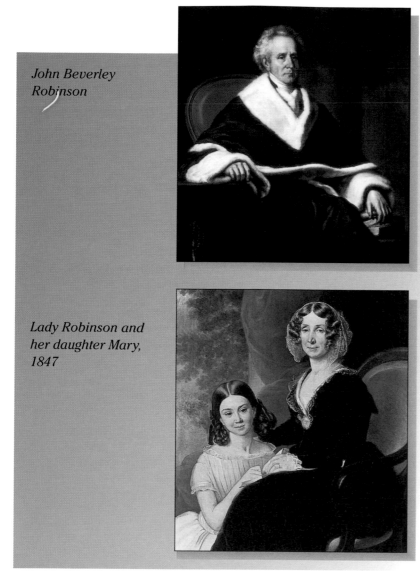

John Beverley Robinson

Lady Robinson and her daughter Mary, 1847

1827, he founded a university that eventually became the University of Toronto.

Another prominent member of the Family Compact was John Beverley Robinson, a lawyer and chief justice of Upper Canada. The Chief Justice is the chief judge and head of the law courts. In this position, Robinson exercised a great deal of power in the councils and with the governor. As long as the Family Compact could persuade the governor to listen to its advice, the elected representatives of the people in the Assembly did not have much say in government.

Government in the British North American Colonies, 1837

GOVERNOR
- appointed by the government in England
- represented the monarch
- always English
- responsible to the British government

EXECUTIVE COUNCIL
- appointed by the governor, with the term of office determined by the governor
- assisted and gave advice to the governor
- greatly influenced a new governor
- controlled by the Family Compact

LEGISLATIVE COUNCIL
- also called the Upper House
- members appointed by the governor for life
- made and passed laws
- executive councillors could also be members of legislative council

LEGISLATIVE ASSEMBLY
- also called the Lower House
- elected by the people for up to 4 years
- made and passed bills
- elections here often influenced by the Family Compact

4. The Problem of Transportation

Farmers need roads to get their products to market, but in Upper Canada the roads were terribly inadequate. For most of the year, even main roads were impassable. Only in winter, when they were frozen over, were many roads easily travelled.

The government, however, did spend large amounts of tax money building canals. But these benefitted the merchant members of the Family Compact and their business friends. Private business people were granted free land and huge loans to build the Welland Canal. This project made passage from Lake Erie to Lake Ontario possible by going around the rapids on the Niagara River and Niagara Falls.

A bush road in Upper Canada, 1842. Can you see why transportation would have been difficult?

To farmers, it seemed that the government granted money to everyone but them. They found it almost impossible to borrow money to buy land, improve their farms, or buy new farm tools. Bankers and merchants grew prosperous, while farmers struggled just to keep their farms going. Thus the lack of a voice in government, no access to influential positions, unfair distribution of land grants, and no money to improve farming conditions were all sparks that burst into the flame of rebellion in 1837.

CHARACTERS IN CANADIAN HISTORY: SUSANNA MOODIE

Susanna Moodie was one of the most famous of the early settlers of Upper Canada. She and her sister, Catharine Parr Traill, were both remarkable authors in the early days of the colony. These pioneer women came to Canada in the 1830s with their husbands. They helped carve their farms out of the wilderness, and wrote about their experiences in these harsh backwoods of Upper Canada. In her most famous book, *Roughing It in the Bush*, published in 1852, Susanna described the struggles of pioneer life.

Susanna Moodie's diaries are also a fascinating source of information about life in Upper Canada. Her husband served with the government troops in putting down the Rebellion of 1837. The following is an excerpt from her diary, written at the time of the Rebellion.

Susanna Moodie

Buried in the obscurity of these woods (north of Peterborough) we knew nothing, heard nothing of the political state of the country, and were little aware of the revolution which was about to work a great change for us and for Canada….

A letter from my sister explained the nature of the outbreak and the astonishment with which the news had been received by all the settlers in the bush. My brother and my sister's husband had already gone off to join some of the numerous bands of gentlemen who were collecting from all quarters to march to the aid of Toronto, which it was said was besieged by the rebel force. She advised me not to permit Moodie to leave home in his present weak state; but the spirit of my husband was aroused, he instantly obeyed what he considered the imperative call of duty, and told me to prepare for him a few necessaries, that he might be ready to start early in the morning…

The honest backwoodsmen, perfectly ignorant of the abuses that had led to the present position of things, regarded the rebels as a set of monsters, for whom no punishment was too severe, and obeyed the call to arms with enthusiasm. The leader of the rebels must have been astonished at the rapidity with which a large force was collected, as if by magic, to put down the rebellion.

DEVELOPING SKILLS: CREATING A MIND MAP

Your class is discussing transportation in nineteenth-century Canada. Most students around you are writing down information in sentences and paragraphs. But your notes consist of sketches of a steam engine, an ox cart, and a horse-drawn sleigh. Don't despair! You have the beginning of a mind map. A **mind map** is a mental picture. It is a way of recording visually what you learn. It is a good way to organize information because it highlights important points, shows how ideas are connected, and triggers or cues your mind to remember information.

A mind map can help you to analyse the major causes of discontent in Upper Canada that led to rebellion in 1837.

■ Step 1: Visual Reminder

Examine the mind map on page 11. Notice that the main idea, "CAUSES OF DISCONTENT," is written in capital letters and is the centre of the diagram. All other ideas are connected to it. Drawing shapes around the ideas or using symbols can help to create a visual reminder of what they mean and show their importance. For example, a sketch of the Parliament Buildings is one way to illustrate "Government."

■ Step 2: Causes

The first cause of discontent listed is "Government." Copy the mind map and fill in the other main causes in capital letters using the information in this chapter as a resource. Include a question mark after each cause to remind you that you need to investigate further. Developing a shape to symbolize each cause helps to make the main idea stand out in your memory.

■ Step 3: Summarize

The information provided under Government presents a visual picture of how the government was organized: the roles and powers of the Assembly, the governor, and the councils, and how government works today. Point-form notes summarize important information and answer the question "How was government a cause of discontent?" Print a few key details under the subtopic heading and draw lines to link the details to the heading. Look at the sample mind map we are creating here. Notice that a map can show at a glance the connections between ideas. For example, our map tells that both **COUNCILS** are **APPOINTED BY THE GOVERNOR**. Also, the circle around **GOVERNOR** and **COUNCILS** indicates that these people were the only ones with the power to pass laws.

■ Step 4: Fill in

Notice the arrows pointing out from the diagram. What do these represent? Fill in the important information to replace the question marks.

■ Step 5: Review

When your mind map is complete, review it and compare it with those of your classmates. Discuss similarities and differences. What is the value of having a visual layout of your notes?

■ Step 6: Discuss

Discuss the following question: "Was any one cause more important than the others as a source of discontent? Why or why not?" Justify your answer.

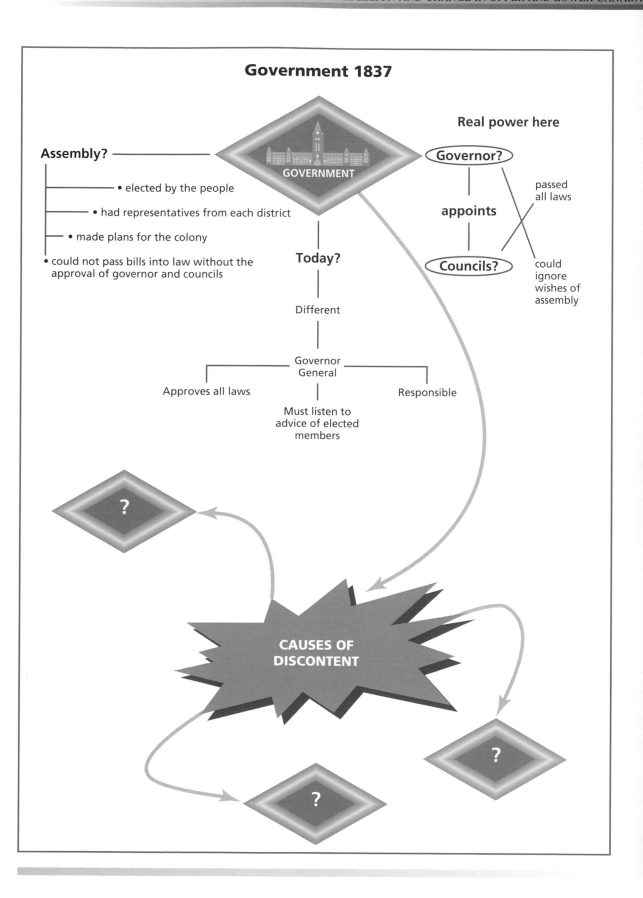

Government 1837

GOVERNMENT

Real power here

Assembly?
- elected by the people
- had representatives from each district
- made plans for the colony
- could not pass bills into law without the approval of governor and councils

Governor?

appoints

Councils?

passed all laws

could ignore wishes of assembly

Today?

Different

Governor General

Approves all laws

Must listen to advice of elected members

Responsible

?

CAUSES OF DISCONTENT

?

?

Tories and Reformers

CHARACTERS IN CANADIAN HISTORY: WILLIAM LYON MACKENZIE

A fiery reformer

The most outspoken reformer in Upper Canada was William Lyon Mackenzie. From the time he arrived in the colony from Scotland in 1820, Mackenzie had been complaining about the government. In York he set up his newspaper, the *Colonial Advocate*. In the *Advocate* he attacked the Family Compact, and even the governor. He printed scandals and gossip about the Family Compact for all the colony to read.

Late one night, some sons of Family Compact members decided to end Mackenzie's attacks upon their parents once and for all. They broke into his newspaper office, smashed his press, and threw the type into the bay. Mackenzie learned the names of the young lawbreakers and brought them to court. He won the case and with the money received from his lawsuit he bought a better press and renewed his attacks on the governor and the Family Compact!

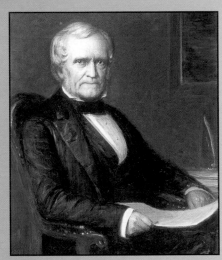

William Lyon Mackenzie

In 1827, Mackenzie was elected to the Assembly, representing the people who lived from Lot Street (now Queen Street) in Toronto north to Lake Simcoe. In the Assembly, Mackenzie continued his fiery attacks on the government. Mackenzie was only 1.65 m tall, but people listened to him when he spoke. It is said that he was completely bald and wore a flaming red wig, which he would sometimes toss into the air in front of the startled Assembly members! Five times Mackenzie was expelled from the Assembly for his attacks on the government. But each time the voters voted him back and the attacks continued. In 1834, when York became the city of Toronto, Mackenzie was chosen its first mayor. He was mayor when the Rebellion of 1837 broke out.

Who Were the Tories?

Friends and supporters of the Family Compact were known as **Conservatives**, or **Tories**. Tories wanted to "conserve," or keep the existing form of government more or less as it was. Conservatives might say, "We don't want any changes. Things are fine as they are right now in the colony." The Tories approved of England's way of governing its colonies and believed that the governor should be responsible only to the king or queen.

Needless to say, members of the councils were nearly always chosen from among Conservatives.

Who Were the Reformers?

Reformers wanted the system of government changed, or "reformed," so that ordinary people would have more influence. **Moderate reformers** might say, "There are many things that are unjust in the colony. However, changes will not happen overnight. We must attack the problem but realize that it may take years to bring about any change."

Reformers believed in **responsible government**. This meant that the governor should carry out the wishes of the majority in the Assembly. They felt it was time for the colonies to manage their own affairs.

Early Reformers included Robert Gourlay, a Scottish settler who had come to Upper Canada in 1819. He opposed the unfair method of granting land and argued the need for roads. Gourlay was arrested and accused of stirring up the settlers. He was then banished from the colony.

Dr. William Baldwin and his son Robert were among the most influential Reformers in Upper Canada. Although the Baldwins were wealthy, well educated members of the Anglican Church, they were not Tories. The Baldwins were strong supporters of reform, although they never entertained any thought of Upper Canada breaking away from Britain. Instead, they developed their own plan for responsible government. They wanted the governor to do what his council advised him to do and to pick his council from the largest party in the Assembly. In this way, the governor would be carrying out the wishes of the largest number of voters. Upper Canada would then have responsible government as it was practised in Britain itself.

Who Were the Radical Reformers?

In time, some of the moderate reformers in Upper Canada grew more radical. A **Radical** might say, "We want changes in our colony and we want them now. We will use all methods to bring about these changes, including violence if necessary."

Mackenzie and other radical reformers began to lose hope that the Assembly would ever gain the right to make its own laws. They began to talk about breaking away from Britain, just as the Americans had done in 1776. When he started talking about **independence**, Mackenzie lost the support of many moderate Reformers. People like Robert Baldwin were as loyal to Britain as the governor himself. They feared that Mackenzie had gone too far!

A New Governor

In 1836, a new governor, Sir Francis Bond Head, arrived in Upper Canada. He knew nothing about Canada and little about politics. But he did consider all Reformers, including Baldwin and the Moderates, to be disloyal traitors to Britain. The Reformers believed that in sending Head as governor, Britain was saying there would be no self-government or reform in the colony.

During the election of 1836, Sir Francis Bond Head did what no Governor-General would dare do today. He went around the colony urging people to vote for the Tories. "A vote for a Reformer," he warned, "is a vote against Britain!" The Tories won the election, and Mackenzie and many other Reformers lost their seats in the Assembly.

Reform leader Robert Baldwin

ELECTIONS IN UPPER CANADA

Elections in Upper Canada were times of great excitement. Only men had the right to vote in the 1830s. They came to the voting centres from farms on foot, horseback, or in winter by sleigh. Each political party set up headquarters, usually in a local tavern or inn. Outside they built platforms, called hustings. Crowds gathered around to hear speeches by the candidates. Heated discussions followed as citizens tried to convince others to vote for their favourite candidate. Whisky, free sandwiches, and even small amounts of cash were used to bribe the voters to support a certain candidate.

There was no such thing as a secret ballot. When it was time to vote, each person climbed onto the hustings to announce who he was voting for. The clerk recorded the vote and everyone knew how he voted. Sometimes, if the crowd did not like the way a person voted, he could end up with a bloody nose or a broken jaw. Sometimes employers watched the way their workers voted and fired those who voted for the wrong candidate!

Since all the voting took place in the open, people were often afraid to vote the way they really wanted. For that reason, in 1874, the government introduced the **secret ballot**, a piece of paper on which citizens could mark down their choice in private.

Fights sometimes broke out at polling places during elections in the early 1800s

Election Day in York, 2 January 1832

Since daybreak, voters had been heading to the Red Lion Inn. An election had been called because there was a vacant seat in the Assembly of Upper Canada. The people's hero, William Lyon Mackenzie, had been thrown out of the Assembly for criticizing the government. Now a by-election was necessary and excitement was in the air.

By ten o'clock that morning, a large crowd had gathered. Mackenzie was ushered onto the hustings to the sound of bagpipes. A loud cheer went up from the crowd. Mackenzie and his Tory opponent, Mr. Street, were introduced to the voters. Each candidate had a chance to make a speech.

Shortly after one o'clock the polls opened and voting began. Person after person mounted the hustings and announced his vote. By three o'clock, 119 votes had been cast for Mackenzie, but only one person had voted for Mr. Street. Street then withdrew from the contest and conceded the election. The crowd that elected Mackenzie pushed into the tavern to celebrate the victory!

After dark, a torchlight parade of sleighs set off with Mackenzie through the streets of York. In front of the Parliament Buildings Mackenzie's supporters let out a defiant cheer. They had re-elected their member, and he would be the people's representative no matter how much it annoyed the governor and the Family Compact!

Mackenzie's Call to Arms

Radical Reformers decided the time had come to take up arms. If reforms could not be attained through peaceful means, they would fight for their beliefs. In late November 1837, Mackenzie published a bold call for independence from Britain:

Canadians! Do you love freedom?...Do you hate oppression? Do you wish perpetual peace?...Then buckle on your armour, and put down the villains who oppress and enslave our country....The bounty you must pay for freedom is to give the strength of your arms to put down tyranny at Toronto.

Up then, brave Canadians! Get ready your rifles and make short work of it;...with governors from England we will have bribery at elections, corruption, villainy, and continued trouble in every township. But Independence would give us the means of enjoying many blessings.

This was Mackenzie's call to arms. In the backwoods and in the Tory stronghold of Toronto, colonists shouldered their muskets. The time had come to overthrow the government of Upper Canada.

As you have read, the rebellion was short-lived as it was put down by Sir Francis Bond Head and Loyalist troops. Mackenzie fled towards the American border at Niagara. For much of the way he travelled on foot. Even with a price of £1000 on his head, his supporters risked their lives to hide him from government search parties. One proud supporter who helped his hero to escape ordered these words to be printed on his own gravestone:

Up the hill stood the home of Samuel Chandler
He guided Mackenzie to Buffalo
And here they had supper
Dec. 10, 1837

Four days later, freezing and exhausted, Mackenzie stepped to safety on American soil.

From Navy Island in the Niagara River, Mackenzie tried to keep his rebellion alive. With 200 supporters he conducted raids along the border. But when officials of Upper Canada protested, the American government arrested Mackenzie and imprisoned him in Rochester for eighteen months.

Two of Mackenzie's leading supporters were not as lucky. Samuel Lount, a blacksmith from Holland Landing, and Peter Matthews, a farmer from Pickering, were captured after several days. They were both convicted and sentenced to hang for their leading roles in the rebellion.

Elizabeth Lount, Samuel's wife, visited the governor and begged for her husband's life. She collected the signatures of 30 000 people who urged the governor to spare the lives of Lount and Matthews. Bond Head refused to accept her pleas, however, and the execution was carried

Elizabeth Lount visits the governor

out at the Toronto jail. Peter Matthews left a widow and fifteen children. Samuel Lount left a widow and seven children. Their bodies were buried in unmarked graves, but were later moved to the Toronto burial ground known as the Necropolis. In 1893, a monument was erected that carries the following inscription:

The monument to Samuel Lount and Peter Matthews

This monument is erected to the memory of Samuel Lount of Holland Landing, County of York, Born 24th September 1791, Died 12th April 1838, and of Peter Matthews of Pickering, County of Ontario, Born 1786, Died 12th April 1838. Erected by their friends and sympathizers, 1893.

Two months after the execution of her husband, Elizabeth Lount wrote, "Canada will do justice to his memory. Canadians cannot long remain in bondage. They will be free." Ninety-two other rebels were sent to a British prison colony in Van Diemen's Land, today called Tasmania, an island state of Australia.

Aftermath of the Rebellion

It is estimated that in the year following the failure of the rebellion, 25 000 disgruntled citizens left Upper Canada for the United States. Their hopes of seeing change in Upper Canada had been dashed. At a time when the total population of Upper Canada was 300 000, the loss of 25 000 citizens was a serious blow to the life and economy of the colony.

Twelve years after the rebellion, Mackenzie was officially pardoned. He returned to Toronto, where he lived until his death in 1861. His daughter Isabel, the youngest of his thirteen children, married John King in 1872. They became parents of a son whom they named William Lyon Mackenzie King, who in 1921 became Canada's eleventh prime minister.

Discontent in Lower Canada

During the 1830s, there was also a growing reform movement in Lower Canada.

In many ways the situation was similar to that of Upper Canada. Many people were dissatisfied with the way in which the colony was governed. The elected Assembly was pulling in one direction, while the two appointed councils were pulling in another. But in Lower Canada, there was an added difficulty. The colony had two languages and cultures: French and English.

Eighty per cent of the citizens in Lower Canada were French speaking and they were the dominant group in the elected Assembly. The French members of the Assembly were angry with the English governor, who rejected their bills to preserve the French language, the Roman Catholic religion, and their traditional agricultural way of life. Most of the governor's appointed councillors were English-speaking merchants and bankers. They were more interested in using the colony's tax money to build roads and canals because these would benefit their business interests.

This was a double insult to the French-speaking population. Not only were they being governed by a few powerful men who had no interest in their concerns

A typical farming area of Lower Canada in the early 1800s. The French-Canadians wanted to preserve their way of life under British rule.

but they were being governed by the English. This ruling group was known as the **Chateau Clique** because they often met at the governor's residence at Chateau St. Louis.

There was another cause of discontent in Lower Canada, however. The English-speaking population was growing so rapidly that the French-speaking people, who were mainly farmers, were beginning to feel outnumbered. In the Eastern Townships near the American border, large numbers of English-speaking settlers were being given land grants. The French feared that there would be no land left for their children to farm in the future. They also resented the growing number of English business people and their domination of industry and commerce in cities like Montreal. The French were afraid that their traditional agricultural way of life would change and that they would soon be swamped by the growing number of English in the colony.

CHARACTERS IN CANADIAN HISTORY: LOUIS-JOSEPH PAPINEAU

Louis-Joseph Papineau

Louis-Joseph Papineau was the leader of the French-speaking Reformers in the Assembly of Lower Canada. The Reformers, or **Patriotes** as they were known in Lower Canada, wanted changes that would give French-speaking people a greater role in lawmaking. They feared that Britain wanted to turn their people into English women and men. Papineau and the Patriotes were dedicated to preserving French language, law, and religion.

While Mackenzie was denouncing the Family Compact in Upper Canada, Papineau was leading attacks on the governor and the powerful English-speaking Chateau Clique. In 1834, the angry Assembly of Lower Canada drew up a document of complaints called the **Ninety-two Resolutions**. The Assembly members threatened to withhold tax money that paid government salaries and was used to build bridges, roads, and canals. Papineau also ordered his supporters not to buy British goods from English merchants. The Assembly hoped these tactics would force the British into listening to their complaints.

Time passed, however, and nothing changed. Papineau and the Patriotes began to suggest that the American system of government would be better. Some talked openly of armed rebellion. But like Mackenzie's reform movement in Upper Canada, the Patriotes lost some of their supporters when they threatened violence. Moderate reformers did not believe that armed rebellion was the way to bring about change. The Roman Catholic Church, too, warned people not to take part in any violence. The situation became so serious that troops were sent from Upper Canada in case of trouble.

In the fall of 1837, Papineau's followers took up arms against the government. Fighting actually broke out in Lower Canada a month before Mackenzie and his rebels marched against Toronto in early December. The timeline illustrates the dramatic events of the rebellion in Lower Canada.

TIMELINE OF A REBELLION—LOWER CANADA, 1837

6 November 1837

Street fighting between French and English breaks out in Montreal. Some English officers, coming out of their club, get into a fight with a group of French Canadian Patriotes. Soon the violence spreads to other parts of Lower Canada. The governor takes no chances and calls to Upper Canada for reinforcements. He is determined to crush the riot before it turns into widespread rebellion.

Patriotes victorious at St. Denis

23 November 1837

A British army, led by Colonel Gore, attacks Patriote headquarters in the village of St. Denis in the hope of capturing Louis-Joseph Papineau. The British meet a strong defence from about 300 armed Patriotes who are holed up behind the thick stone walls of the village houses. Church bells ring out the alarm. Soon Patriote reinforcements begin to arrive from the surrounding countryside. After seven hours of fighting, government troops are forced to withdraw. It is a Patriote victory!

British defeat rebels at St. Charles

25 November 1837

Two days after their defeat at St. Denis, a large force of government troops raids another Patriote stronghold at St. Charles. The town is burned and at least forty rebels are killed. Patriotes blame their defeat on their worn-out guns and the fact that they were outnumbered two to one.

14 December 1837

Rebellion quelled at St. Eustache

Two thousand troops and Loyalist volunteers attack the village of St. Eustache. The Patriotes have fortified themselves inside the village church. The troops set fire to the church. More than seventy Patriotes are shot as they flee from the burning building. Later the town is looted. Families are turned out of their homes to freeze in the snow. The rebellion in Lower Canada is over. Patriote resistance is overcome and the rebels scatter for fear of arrest. Papineau, under the name of Mr. Louis, flees to the United States.

Why the Rebellion Failed

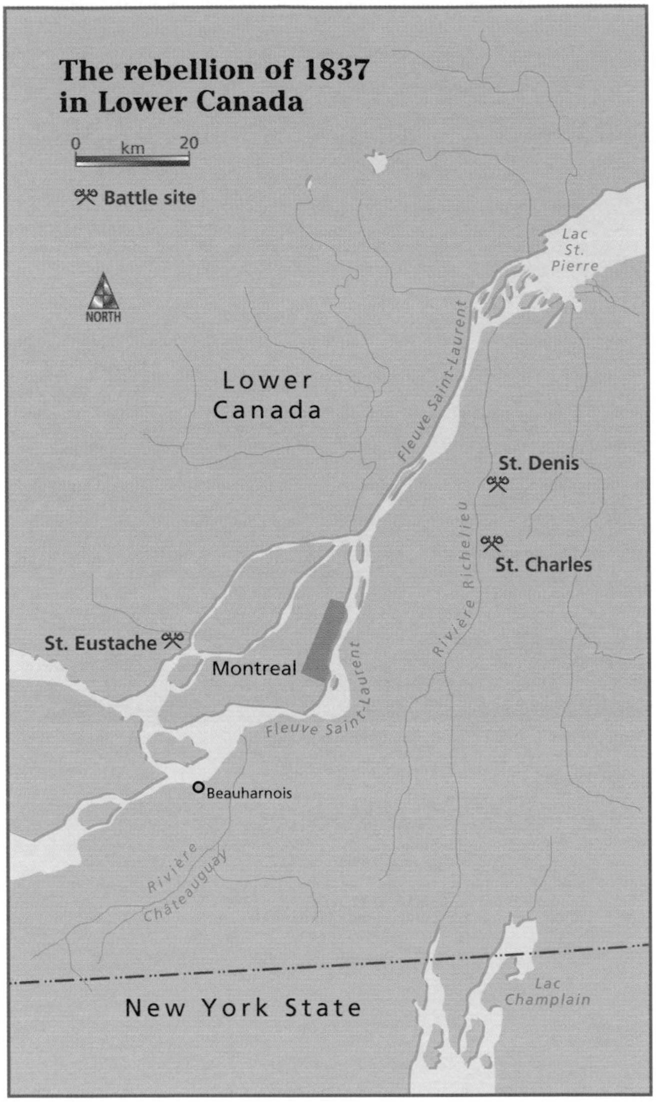
The rebellion of 1837 in Lower Canada
0 km 20
Battle site
NORTH
Lac St. Pierre
Lower Canada
Fleuve Saint-Laurent
St. Denis
St. Charles
Rivière Richelieu
St. Eustache
Montreal
Fleuve Saint-Laurent
Beauharnois
Rivière Châteauguay
New York State
Lac Champlain

The Patriotes and their rebellion in Lower Canada failed for two main reasons. The first was a lack of planning and military leadership. Politicians could inspire the people with words, but they did not have the skills to plan a battle. Furthermore, only one in ten Patriotes had a gun. They were not trained soldiers, so they were no match against British troops. The second reason the rebellion failed was because the Roman Catholic Church did not approve of armed rebellion. Therefore, many Patriotes, unwilling to go against the wishes of their church, simply refused to join the rebellion.

In 1838, Papineau's more radical followers attempted another rebellion, but it was crushed within a few days. Afterwards, Papineau sailed for Paris, where he remained until he was pardoned by the governor in 1845. He returned to Quebec, where he died in 1871 at the age of eighty-five.

Responsible Government at Last

Lord Durham's Report

After the rebellions in Upper and Lower Canada, the British government realized that something had to be done. For years the colonists in Upper and Lower Canada had expressed their dissatisfaction with the way they were governed. Britain had ignored their complaints, but now it could no longer sit back and do nothing. Recent armed rebellions in both colonies convinced the British that it was time to take action.

The British government sent Lord Durham to Canada as Governor-in-Chief of all of the British North American colonies. His task was to report on the troubles and suggest reforms. Lord Durham set to work to find out as much about British North America as he could.

Rebels at Beauharnois, Lower Canada, a village southwest of Montreal. Painted by an eyewitness of the event, Katherine Jane Ellice, 1838.

He sent officials throughout the colonies to talk with ordinary people in the towns and with settlers in the backwoods. He went to Toronto himself to meet Robert Baldwin and other Reformers who had been struggling for better government in the colony. After five months, Lord Durham addressed the troubles in the colonies in his famous **Durham Report.**

Lord Durham made two main recommendations. The first was that the two colonies of Upper and Lower Canada should be joined into one province of Canada. The second was that responsible government should be granted to British North America. Lord Durham suggested that the advisors to the governor should always be chosen from the largest party in the elected Assembly and that the governor must sign all bills the Assembly passed.

Lord Durham's report contained other suggestions as well. He recommended that the Anglican Church should have no more privileges than any other Protestant church. The colonies should be allowed to manage their own day-to-day affairs and settle local matters. The British government should focus its attention on issues affecting the British Empire, such as defence, and constitutional reform in the colonies. Lord Durham also suggested that one day all of the British North American colonies might be joined together.

One of Durham's recommendations was especially controversial. He decided that the rebellion in Lower Canada was much more than a protest against unjust government. He felt it was a power strug-

Lord Durham in British North America

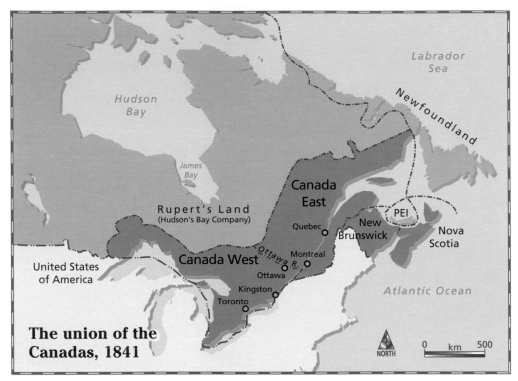

The union of the Canadas, 1841

Hudson Bay

James Bay

Labrador Sea

Newfoundland

Rupert's Land
(Hudson's Bay Company)

Canada East

Quebec

PEI

New Brunswick

Nova Scotia

Ottawa R.

Montreal

Canada West

Ottawa

Kingston

Toronto

United States of America

Atlantic Ocean

NORTH

0   km   500

gle between the French and the English. Uniting Upper and Lower Canada would be one way of solving the conflict. Durham concluded that French-Canadians should be forced to speak English and practise English values. In a united province, the English-speaking colonists would be the majority. Living side-by-side with the English, the French would eventually learn the English language and English values. What Durham failed to understand or appreciate, however, was how deeply French-Canadians treasured their own language, traditions, and way of life.

On Lord Durham's advice, Upper and Lower Canada were united by the **Act of Union** in 1841. Upper Canada became known as Canada West and Lower Canada was renamed Canada East. The new government first met at Kingston before the capital of the united colonies was moved to Montreal.

Lord Durham's recommendation for responsible government was not granted until 1848. At that time, the British government began to look more favourably upon the idea of allowing the colonies to govern themselves.

The Arrival of Lord Elgin

In 1846, a new Governor-General was appointed to Canada. He was Lord Elgin,

Lord Elgin

the son-in-law of Lord Durham. Elgin agreed with Lord Durham's idea that the colonies should be allowed to govern themselves and supported the idea of responsible government.

In the election of 1848, more Reformers than Tories were elected to the Assembly. Lord Elgin asked the Reform leaders, Robert Baldwin (Canada West) and Louis Lafontaine (Canada East), to recommend which elected officials should advise him. They, of course, chose Assembly members from the Reform party. Lord Elgin promised that he would take their advice as long as the Reformers held a majority in the Assembly. Responsible government had arrived!

The Rebellion Losses Bill

A showdown between the Reformers and the Tories was lurking in 1849. The **Rebellion Losses Bill** proposed that money should be paid to people in Lower Canada whose property had been damaged during the rebellion. They would receive compensation for damage to their homes, barns, fences, livestock, wagons, and other personal property.

Upper Canadians had already received similar compensation. The Tories voted against the bill because they were concerned that former rebels would be paid for losses they suffered during their rebellion. They insisted that no rebels should be rewarded for their actions and that to do so might lead to violence between the two sides. But the Reformers had the largest number of members in the Assembly, so the Tories were outvoted. The bill was passed and sent to Lord Elgin to be signed into law.

Lord Elgin's Dilemma

In his carriage on the way to Parliament, Lord Elgin knew that he was faced with an important decision. He would be asked to approve the Rebellion Losses Bill. He did not think the bill was wise and he was reluctant to pass it into law. But the government of Baldwin and Lafontaine favoured the bill, and the elected representatives of the people had passed it.

What should Lord Elgin do? The elected representatives of the people had spoken. He was following the advice of

The Parliament of the united Canadas opened in Montreal, 1844. The Assembly met in various cities until Ottawa became the permanent capital in 1857.

the leaders with a majority of supporters in the Assembly. But the thought of violence was disturbing. Lord Elgin's wife, Lady Mary, was about to give birth and he feared that an attack on the governor's mansion might threaten his wife and unborn child. On the other hand, Mary was the daughter of Lord Durham, who had originally suggested self-government for the colonies. Lady Mary supported the ideas of her father and urged her husband to sign the bill.

DEVELOPING SKILLS: DECISION MAKING

You have probably come up against some tough decisions in your life, and there are more ahead of you! Can you join a club or sports team and still keep up your grades? What should you do to find a summer job? What career should you pursue? Often, these decisions can be easier to work through if you follow a careful reasoning process.

Let's take an example. Suppose you have a friend who you know has been shoplifting. You want to help her.

■ Step 1: Problem Statement

First, state the problem as a question. It should begin with something like, "In what ways might ...?", or "How might ...?", or How should ...?" Try out a few problem statements and choose the one that is most relevant and meaningful.

Sample question:

"How should we help our friend with her shoplifting problem?"

■ Step 2: Brainstorm

Brainstorm alternative solutions to the problem. Try to generate as many ideas as you can, even if they seem outrageous at first.

Alternatives:

- Ask a teacher whom you trust for advice.
- Persuade your friend to see a counsellor.
- Tell your friend's parents.
- Talk with your friend about her problem.
- Go with your friend to her parents or a counsellor.
- Don't do anything.

■ Step 3: Criteria

You have no doubt produced more alternative solutions than you can deal with. You need some basis for making your decision, some way of working out what is important to you in this situation. In other words, you need criteria by which to judge. List criteria that you think are important in evaluating your alternative solutions.

Criteria:

- The friendship is maintained.
- Your friend gets help.
- As few people as possible know about the problem.
- Your friend stays out of trouble.
- Your friend is not suspended from school.
- Your friend feels supported .
- The solution does not cost too much.
- The solution is practical.
- Your friend maintains her dignity.

■ Step 4: Solutions

Choose five of your most promising solutions and your five most important criteria. Now you need to evaluate your alternative solutions according to your criteria. Write your criteria and your alternatives in a matrix like the one on page 25.

■ Step 5: Rank

Rank each of your alternatives from 1 through 5 on the first criterion. Score 5 for the best and 1 for the poorest solution. Next, rank each alternative on the second criterion in the same way. Continue until you have ranked all your alternative ideas according to your criteria. Make sure all the numbers from 1 to 5 are used in each column. Now total the numbers for each alternative. Which alternative scores highest?

■ Step 6: Decide

State your decision and make a plan for how you would carry it out.

■ Step 7: Evaluate

Evaluate your decision. If your plan were carried out, what would be the desired results?

Criteria	Alternatives				
	1 Get advice from a teacher	2 Talk with your friend	3 Tell her parents	4 Persuade her to see a counsellor	5 Go with her to a counsellor
Friendship is maintained	4	1	5	3	2
Friend gets help					
Friend feels supported					
Friend stays out of trouble					
As few people as possible know					
Total					

Try It!

Now you can use this model to help you decide what you would do if you were Lord Elgin. Would you sign the Rebellion Losses Bill?

In groups, follow the steps in the decision-making process. Come to a group decision on this issue and present it to the class. Discuss the usefulness of the decision-making model. Then turn to the text to discover what Lord Elgin decided to do.

Lord Elgin's Decision

When the bill was handed to him, Lord Elgin signed it immediately. What happened next was recorded by Rufus Seaver, an eyewitness, in a letter to his wife.

Montreal, April 25th, 1849

My dear wife:

I begin by saying that I am glad you and the children are not here, for we are on the eve of another rebellion….It is rumoured that the Rebellion Losses Bill was now to be signed. The report spread through town like wildfire. An immense mob assembled and surrounded Parliament to see what the Governor intended to do. When it was finally announced that he had signed the bill, there was trouble.

As his Excellency, the Governor, left Parliament, he was struck with stones, chips, and rotten and good eggs thrown by thousands of people. He was struck in the face with an egg, his carriage windows were broken, but by the speed of his horses, he was able to escape with no injury except to his carriage.

I stop here, for the cry is raised that Parliament is on fire. "Fire!" is the cry. From my door, I can see the red flames lighting up the heavens—I go— more news after I see what the fuss is about.

April 26th, 1849

It is too true. Last night about eight o'clock, while Parliament was still sitting, a mob assembled and commenced the destruction of the building by breaking windows. (It can be called nothing but a mob, though composed of some of our most worthy Tory citizens.) Soon the doors were broken open and…fires were lit in a dozen places….Members barely escaped with their lives.

Your affectionate husband,

Wm. Rufus Seaver

Burning of the Parliament House in Montreal, 1849

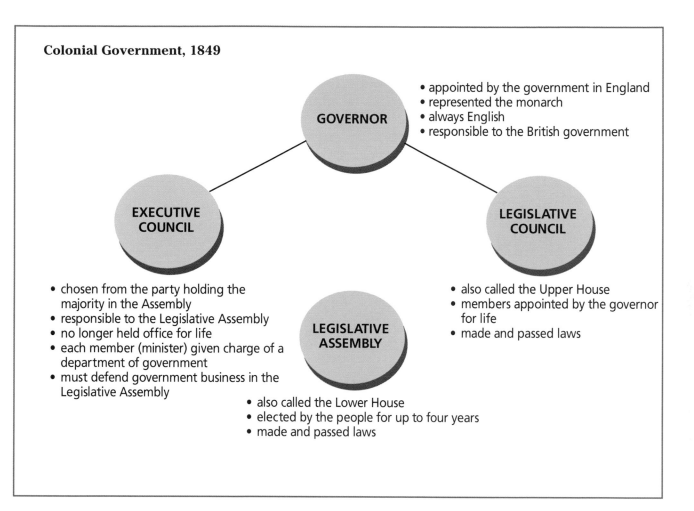

Colonial Government, 1849

GOVERNOR
- appointed by the government in England
- represented the monarch
- always English
- responsible to the British government

EXECUTIVE COUNCIL
- chosen from the party holding the majority in the Assembly
- responsible to the Legislative Assembly
- no longer held office for life
- each member (minister) given charge of a department of government
- must defend government business in the Legislative Assembly

LEGISLATIVE ASSEMBLY
- also called the Lower House
- elected by the people for up to four years
- made and passed laws

LEGISLATIVE COUNCIL
- also called the Upper House
- members appointed by the governor for life
- made and passed laws

Five days later, as Lord Elgin drove into Montreal, he was once again attacked by Tories. In 1837, it had been the other way around as Tories had rushed to support Governor Bond Head in putting down the rebels. Now Tories were attacking the British governor, the representative of the queen!

In order to carry out the wishes of the elected representatives of the people and to give them responsible government, Lord Elgin twice risked his life by facing angry mobs. His carriage was badly damaged by rocks and bricks hurled at it. But Lord Elgin never had it fixed. He wanted people to see it and remember at what price responsible government had been won.

How Citizens Can Influence Government Today

Many Canadians take their rights for granted. We have the right to speak out and criticize our government. We have the right to practise any religion or none at all. We are free to travel outside Canada whenever we wish. We have the right to live and work in any province in Canada. These rights, and many others, are guaranteed in the Charter of Rights and Freedoms. However, rights impose obligations. If you have the right to freely express your ideas, then you have the obligation to let others freely express theirs.

Obligations and Opportunities of Citizenship

Obligation: Get Involved

Elections give you a chance to participate in the governing of your country and in the choice of the government. Yet federal and provincial elections sometimes draw about 60 per cent of voters. In municipal elections, the turnout may be as low as 30 per cent. In some cases, victory is decided by only a few votes, which means that every vote counts.

Ideal voters are informed voters. They examine the different parties and candidates. They know the issues and cast their votes only after careful thought. One way to become a well-informed voter is to get involved in a political party. You can participate more fully in an election by contributing your time, labour, and money to the political party of your choice. Some day you might even consider becoming a candidate for election!

Opportunity: Write Your Member of Parliament

Citizens have the right to make their opinions and ideas known to their elected representatives. Politicians can do a better job when they know their constituents' views. In 1987, for example, the House of Commons held a **free debate** on capital punishment. A free debate allows MPs to vote according to their conscience and not by party policy. In the months leading up to the debate, thousands of citizens wrote to their MPs expressing their views. After the vote, commentators said that one of the decisive factors influencing the vote was the well-organized letter-writing campaign by opponents of the death penalty. These people used their influence and power to convince enough MPs to defeat the motion calling for a return to capital punishment.

Opportunity: Speak to a Parliamentary Committee

On controversial and important issues, governments sometimes establish special parliamentary committees. Members of the committee, or task force, travel from place to place listening to the views of average citizens. Based on these opinions, the task force makes recommendations to the government. Appearing before a parliamentary committee offers an opportunity to have direct influence on government policy.

Opportunity: Join a Pressure Group

We have examined how an individual can influence the decision-making process. If individuals join forces, they have even more power.

Suppose a group of neighbours is concerned about plans to open a dump site in their area. They decide to support the mayoral candidate who opposes dump sites near residential areas. Their support helps to ensure that their candidate wins the election.

Pressure groups can do a number of things to express their opinions and influence government decision making. They can **lobby** people in government—that is, make personal contacts with government officials to express the ideas and goals of their interest group. Another way to apply pressure is to use the media to get the public's attention. Greenpeace, for example, used the media to focus worldwide attention on the seal hunt off Canada's east coast. Millions of people who saw pictures of cute baby harp seals being killed refused to purchase products made from the seal pelts. By 1984, the market for pelts had declined drastically.

In response, aboriginal leaders from Canada, the United States, and Greenland joined forces with the fur industry. They formed their own pressure group to lobby the government and media to tell their side of the story. The group explained how the anti-trapping movement was threatening their existence. They said that the traditional methods used by aboriginal peoples to hunt seals were not inhumane. They hoped that if the public understood the other side of the seal hunt issue, they would drop their opposition.

Opportunity: Participate in Peaceful Demonstrations

Sometimes demonstrations and protest meetings are the only ways to attract a government's attention. Peaceful demonstrations and large meetings not only bring a cause to the attention of the legislators, but to other Canadians as well. This increases the pressure on governments to take action.

Environmental activists waged a battle with logging companies at Clayoquot Sound on Vancouver Island. Their campaign protested plans to cut the largest patch of temperate rainforest left in British Columbia. They staged anti-logging demonstrations in Canada and internationally. By the summer of 1994, the premier of British Columbia announced a plan to reduce logging on Vancouver Island and designate 13 per cent of the island as parkland. Although the decision eliminated about 900 logging jobs over five years, the premier said that international pressure and boycott left him little choice.

A Greenpeace worker spraying a baby harp seal with paint to make the pelt worthless to sealers

Several demonstrations were held against logging in Clayoquot Sound. How effective were these campaigns?

ACTIVITIES

Check Your Understanding

1. Start a *Factfile* on Canadian history. This *Factfile* will be your personal file of key terms, their meanings, and their historical importance. Set aside a section of your notebook for your *Factfile* or create it on a computer. You will be adding to your file as you encounter new terms throughout your study. Refer to your *Factfile* for quick reference any time you need a reminder about some key information.
   a) Divide the pages in your notebook or on your computer into three columns. Make the middle column the widest.
   b) In the left column, write the key term. In the middle column, write a definition or description of the term. If you can, include a picture, sketch, or computer graphic to help you describe the term.
   c) In the third column, write a brief point-form note about the historical importance of the term. Start your *Factfile* with the following terms:

   • change • Assembly • Clergy Reserves • conflict • bill • governor • rebellion • Executive council • Legislative council • United Empire Loyalist • Family Compact • secret ballot • Tory • Reformer • Moderate Reformer • Radical • responsible government • Patriote •Chateau Clique • Ninety-two Resolutions • Durham Report • Rebellion Losses Bill • Act of Union 1841.

2. a) What were the rights and privileges held by the members of the Family Compact?
   b) Why did the governor rely so heavily on the Family Compact for advice?
   c) Why did the elected Assembly in the colonies have little real power?

3. Using an organizer, indicate what a Radical Reformer, a Moderate Reformer, and a Tory would say about:
   a) their feelings towards Britain
   b) who should run the government
   c) change.

4. How did Robert Baldwin propose to alter the system of government in Upper Canada? Why would Britain find Baldwin's approach more acceptable than Mackenzie's approach?

5. Why did many Patriotes refuse to take up arms against the government?

6. Read the Wanted Poster for William Lyon Mackenzie on page 4.
   a) What would a citizen have to do to claim the £1000 reward?
   b) What else does this poster promise a rebel who turns over William Lyon Mackenzie to the government?
   c) The poster urges people who are followers of Mackenzie to give up the idea of rebellion. What are the three things the poster says the government expects these people to do? What does the government promise in return?

d) On Thursday, 7 December 1837 at 3:00 p.m., what were the rebels doing? What was the government trying to do at this time?

7. What were the two main recommendations of Lord Durham's Report? How and when did the British government respond to these recommendations?

8. Why was the signing of the Rebellion Losses Bill a dilemma for Lord Elgin?

Confirm Your Learning

9. Develop an organizer to compare the rebellions in Upper and Lower Canada. Use the following criteria in your comparison:
   a) causes of discontent
   b) leadership
   c) support from the people
   d) battles won/lost
   e) results in government, for the leaders, for the participants, and for the people of the two Canadas.

10. Was the hanging of Samuel Lount justified? Explain your answer.

11. From which of the following occupational and geographical areas did Mackenzie receive the most support in the Rebellion of 1837? Suggest reasons for this.

Arrests by Occupation

small landowner or farmer	374
labourer	345
craft worker	72
hired farm hand	20
merchant	16
innkeeper	11
medical doctor	8
teacher	4
clerk	4
member of Parliament, former member of Parliament, or son of same	4
gentleman	3
attorney	3
unlicensed medical doctor	3
land surveyor	3
bookseller	3
artist	2
preacher	2
magistrate or son of same	2
engineer	1
mariner	1
law student	1
unknown	3
TOTAL	885

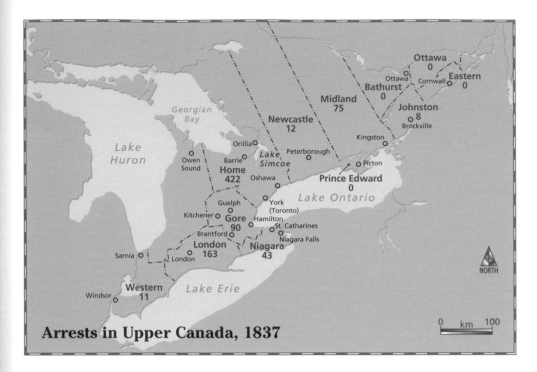

Arrests in Upper Canada, 1837

12. If you had been living in Lower Canada in 1837, on which side would you have fought in the rebellion? Why? Create a poster expressing your position. Imagine that the poster will be seen and read throughout the colony.

Challenge Your Mind

13. Discuss Elizabeth Lount's comments about the rebels: "Canadians cannot long remain in bondage. They will be free."

14. What would be the reaction of the following groups to the recommendations made by Lord Durham?
    a) Tories in Upper and Lower Canada
    b) French-speaking people in Lower Canada
    c) English-speaking people in Lower Canada
    d) Reformers in Upper and Lower Canada
    e) Protestants other than Anglicans in Upper Canada.

15. An interesting historical exercise is to play the "what if" game. "What if" Mackenzie and his supporters had decided to move against Toronto at the exact same time as the outbreak of rebellion in Lower Canada instead of a few weeks later? Would the British have diverted a large portion of their troops back to Upper Canada? Would this have given the French-Canadian revolutionaries a greater chance of victory? Would the history of the rebellion have turned out differently? Would the history of Canada have turned out differently? Discuss the possibilities in groups and present your ideas on what might have happened.

16. Discuss which causes of discontent in Lower Canada in 1837 are still creating unrest in Quebec today. Start a collection of newspaper or magazine articles

about modern Quebec that shows why some of the people in that province are dissatisfied.

17. During the fighting at St. Eustache, Dr. Jean-Olivier Chenier, a Patriote leader, leapt from a church window and died fighting the government troops. After the battle, the government troops cut out Chenier's heart and displayed it in a tavern for several days. In the October Crisis of 1970 in Quebec, the FLQ (Front de libération du Québec) members who kidnapped and killed Pierre Laporte called themselves the "Chenier cell" of the FLQ, after Dr. Chenier. Do some further research on the FLQ crisis in Quebec in 1970. Suggest reasons why the FLQ members might name themselves after Dr. Jean-Olivier Chenier.

18. In what ways were the rebellions of 1837 military failures but political successes?

19. Hold a class discussion on the topic "Were the rebels justified in taking up arms against the official government?" Here are some questions to guide your discussion:
   a) Why do people rebel or riot against a government? Think of recent uprisings you have read about or seen on news reports.
   b) What are the advantages and disadvantages of using violence to express discontent? What methods could people use instead of violence?
   c) Would you be prepared to risk your life to bring about a change in government? Why or why not?
   d) Is there any form of government you would oppose strongly enough to actively fight against it? Why?
   e) Are there any issues at all that are important enough that you would risk your life fighting for them? What are they and why are they so important?
   f) Are riots and rebellions always successful in bringing about change? What are the costs and benefits?

20. Read the following statements carefully. Choose the one that comes closest to describing your point of view about using rebellion to bring about change. Write a short paragraph to explain your viewpoint.
   a) Citizens are entitled to rebel against their government if they don't like it.
   b) Citizens should rebel against the government only as a last resort.
   c) Citizens never have the right to take up arms against the government.

21. Some Canadians have suggested that the right to vote should be taken away from citizens who do not vote in each election. In Australia, a different solution to low voter turnout has been tried. The eligible voters who do not vote in each election are fined. Debate this statement: Everyone in Canada should be required to vote.

CHAPTER 2

The Road to Confederation

CONFEDERATION DAY—1 JULY 1867

The bells started to ring at midnight. Early in the morning guns roared a salute from Halifax in the east to Sarnia in the west. Bonfires and fireworks lit up the sky in cities and towns across the new country. It was the birthday of the Dominion of Canada and the people of New Brunswick, Nova Scotia, Ontario, and Quebec were celebrating.

It was a day of blue skies and sunshine. People of all religious faiths gathered to offer prayers for the future of the nation and its people. Through the crowded streets of Ottawa, the new prime minister, John A. Macdonald, and his government made their way to the Parliament Buildings. There, the new governor-general, Lord Monck, was sworn into office. A royal proclamation was read declaring that the British North America Act was now in effect. Cheers went up for Canada and Queen Victoria. Banners everywhere proclaimed "Good Luck to Confederation!" and "Bienvenue à la Nouvelle Puissance!"

Confederation celebrations in Ottawa, Ontario, 1 July 1867

Factors Leading to Confederation

What events led to this celebration of a new nation on 1 July 1867? The idea of a union, or **confederation**, of all the British colonies in North America had been talked about for many years. Lord Durham had dreamed about some day uniting all the colonies under a central government. In the 1860s, six major factors provided the final push for Confederation.

1. War and Expansionism in the United States

From 1861 to 1865, the United States was embroiled in a civil war. A **civil war** is a war between people who live in the same country. In the **American Civil War**, the Northern states were fighting the Southern states. The issue was whether North and South should remain united or separate into two countries. By 1865, the North had won the war and the United States remained one country.

The American Civil War had nothing to do with Canada or Britain directly. But wars have a habit of affecting many countries. During the American Civil War, Britain appeared to support the Southern states. British shipyards built armed cruisers for sale to the South. One of these, the

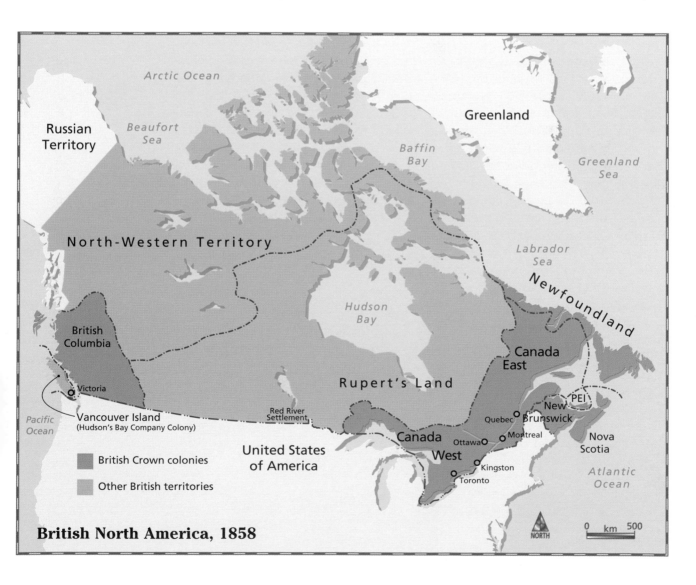

British North America, 1858

Russian Territory

Arctic Ocean

Beaufort Sea

Greenland

Baffin Bay

Greenland Sea

North-Western Territory

Labrador Sea

Newfoundland

British Columbia

Hudson Bay

Victoria

Rupert's Land

Canada East

Vancouver Island
(Hudson's Bay Company Colony)

Pacific Ocean

Red River Settlement

Quebec

New Brunswick

PEI

United States of America

Canada West

Ottawa

Montreal

Nova Scotia

British Crown colonies

Kingston

Atlantic Ocean

Other British territories

Toronto

NORTH

0 km 500

Alabama, captured and destroyed sixty-five Northern ships. The North demanded that Britain pay damages. After the war, Britain paid over $15 million to the United States to settle the claims.

Another incident almost drew Britain into the war directly. It occurred when a Northern ship stopped a British vessel, the *Trent*. Northerners went aboard and took two Southerners prisoner. The British government was angry and insulted to have its vessel stopped and boarded. It might have led to war, but Queen Victoria persuaded the British government to accept an apology instead.

When the North won the war in 1865, the British North American colonies were worried. With the tense relations between Britain and the Northern states, the colonies wondered whether the North would now turn its vast victorious armies against them. Would Americans attack the British North American colonies as a way of taking revenge on Britain?

A number of American newspapers and politicians had been talking about the takeover of Britain's territories to the north. Some Americans believed in **Manifest Destiny**—that is, they believed it was natural that the United States would one day expand to control all of North America. They assumed that before long the whole northern continent would belong to the United States.

In 1867, the United States purchased Alaska from the Russians. Some British North Americans feared the United States would take over the empty plains northwest of Canada next. American settlers, railways, and trade were steadily pressing in on the Red River Settlement near what is now Winnipeg. It looked as if the colony might be surrounded and become so American that it would be joined to the United States.

On the west coast of North America the same thing was happening. The discovery of gold in British Columbia drew thousands of Americans into that colony. Now that the Americans owned Alaska, British Columbia was hemmed in to the north and south by the United States. If the colony of British Columbia and the northwestern plains were to be kept British, something would have to be done quickly. The fear of an American takeover was one factor drawing the colonies together.

2. Fenian Raids

The British North American colonies were actually raided by Irish American troops after the Civil War. These troops were members of an organization called the **Fenians,** who were hostile towards Britain. The Fenians were some of a large number of Irish who had settled in the United States to get away from British rule. At this time, Britain controlled all of Ireland.

In the United States, the Fenians continued to look for a way to free Ireland from British rule. They believed that if they captured the British North American

Fenian raid volunteers.

The Battle of Ridgeway. Fenians carry the Irish flag as they clash with British regulars and militia.

colonies, they might force Britain to free Ireland. Many Fenians were experienced soldiers who had just been released from the victorious Northern army.

The Fenians planned to invade the colonies at a number of points: at Niagara, along the St. Lawrence River, along the New Brunswick-Maine border, and in the Eastern Townships of Canada East. In May 1866, 1500 Fenians crossed the border at Buffalo. They captured Fort Erie and won a victory over a Canadian force at Ridgeway. Six Canadians were killed and thirty were wounded.

When reinforcements failed to arrive, the Fenians turned back across the border. The same year, British warships prevented a Fenian attack in New Brunswick. For the next several years, people living along the border were always on the alert for Fenians, and raids did occur at several points.

The Fenian attacks had two major effects on the British North American colonies. First, John A. Macdonald turned the raids into an argument for union of the colonies. He asserted that a united country would be better able to resist such invasions. Second, there was a growing feeling of resentment against the United States. Many people in the colonies felt that American newspapers encouraged the Fenians. They believed that the United States government should have stopped them at the border. Thus the Fenians provided another push towards Confederation.

3. Trouble with Trade

Another concern to the British North American colonies was the problem of trade. Before 1846, the colonies had enjoyed a special trading relationship with Britain. Britain allowed wheat and flour from the colonies to enter its ports with a low tax. This special favour was called a **preference**. But suddenly, in 1846, Britain cancelled the preference and established free trade. Now Britain would allow goods from any country into its markets without a tax.

Britain's new free trade policy caused serious problems for the economy of the British North American colonies. The colonies would no longer have a guaranteed market in Britain. They would have to find new trading partners. The most obvious choice was their rapidly expanding neighbour to the south, the United States.

In 1854, the British North American colonies signed a **Reciprocity Treaty** with the United States. Reciprocity is an agreement between countries allowing trade in certain goods without tariffs or taxes. By the treaty, it was agreed that the United States could fish along the shores of Atlantic Canada and that British North Americans could fish in some US waters. Both countries would allow the products of farms, mines, and the sea to cross the border tax free. Fish, timber, grain, and cattle were sent to the United States, while American coal and pork were sent north. The treaty was for a ten-year trial period. After that, either side could break the bargain.

During the 1860s, the colonies began to worry that the United States might end the Reciprocity Treaty. Americans were saying they were losing money by allowing British North American goods into their country tax free. They were also upset because Britain had supported the South during the Civil War. In 1865, the United States announced that it intended to end the Reciprocity Treaty.

The British North American colonies were thrown into a panic. The only solution seemed to be free trade among themselves. To this point, there had been little trading among the colonies. When they did exchange goods, they always charged high tariffs. When wheat was

Macdonald favoured reciprocity in 1855 but opposed it in 1888. This cartoon introduces the two Macdonalds.

sent from Canada into the United States, it crossed tax free into that foreign country. But when wheat was shipped to New Brunswick or Nova Scotia, it was taxed! If the colonies were united, it would be easier for them to trade with one another.

4. The Need for Rail Links

If there was to be trade among the colonies, there had to be a railway link. In 1850, British North America had only 106 km of track. Much of the rail business was going to the American railways. It was time, the colonists thought, to build their own railways.

Between 1850 and 1867, 3570 km of track were added in the colonies. The most ambitious railway project was the **Grand Trunk Railway**. It was to be an all-British route linking Canada West with the Atlantic Ocean at Halifax. By 1860, the Grand Trunk had stretched from

A floating dam used in the construction of the Grand Trunk Railway

A railway connection with the Maritime colonies was essential for the defence of British North America. If the colonies were attacked by the United States during the winter, the St. Lawrence River would be blocked by ice. There would be no way British troops could get to the colonies from Halifax by rail without crossing through the United States. It was another reason for Confederation.

Sarnia only as far east as Rivière du Loup in Québec. It cost a tremendous amount of money to build and was on the verge of bankruptcy.

Many people thought that the only way the Grand Trunk could be completed to Halifax was if the colonies were united. Then expenses could be shared. The railways would also provide a communication and trade link among the colonies. Some even dreamed of one day extending the railway right across the continent to British Columbia and the Pacific Ocean.

5. Changing British Attitudes

In England, a small but vocal group called the **Little Englanders** believed the colonies were a great burden to Britain. One of the biggest expenses of colonies was their defence. The Little Englanders felt it was time that the British North American colonies became independent and paid their own way.

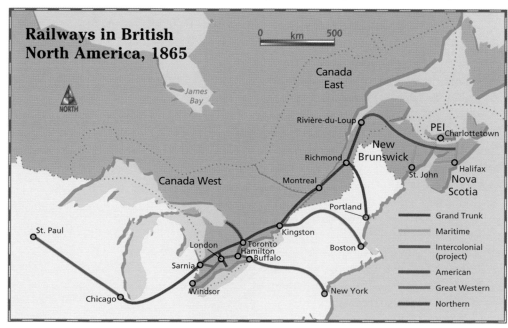

Railways in British North America, 1865

0   km   500

James Bay

NORTH

Canada East

Canada West

Rivière-du-Loup

Richmond

New Brunswick

PEI
Charlottetown

St. John   Halifax

Montreal

Nova Scotia

Portland

St. Paul

Kingston

London
Toronto
Hamilton
Buffalo

Boston

Sarnia

Windsor

Chicago

New York

— Grand Trunk
— Maritime
— Intercolonial (project)
— American
— Great Western
— Northern

Many people in Britain agreed with the Little Englanders. This was bad news for the colonies. It came at the very time that the Fenians were raiding their borders and Americans were threatening to expand into the West. The views of the Little Englanders also helped to push the colonies towards Confederation.

6. Political Deadlock in the Canadas

In the united Canada of the 1860s, the government and the opposition were so nearly even in number that it was almost impossible to get any bills passed through the Assembly or to make any new laws. The machinery of government gradually ground to a halt. It was **political deadlock**.

How had this come about? When Upper and Lower Canada were united in 1841, each part of the new colony was given an equal number of seats in the Assembly. In the beginning, this was unfair to Canada East because more people lived there than in Canada West. Naturally, the people of Canada East protested that they should have more seats in the Assembly on the basis of their population. This was known as **representation by population**.

By 1861, however, immigration had brought so many English-speaking people to Upper Canada that they outnumbered the French-speaking population of Lower Canada by 300 000. Now Canada West was demanding representation by population and Canada East was resisting. The political deadlock continued.

Between 1849 and 1864 there were twelve different governments in power, almost one a year! No government could win enough seats to get anything done. Political deadlock had brought the government to a standstill.

On 14 June 1864, Macdonald's gov-

ernment was defeated by two votes. Macdonald could call an election, but another election would probably change nothing. Neither side could hope to win enough seats in the Assembly to get any bills passed. It was George Brown, leader of the Clear Grits, or Reform Party, who saved the day. Brown suggested that the answer to political deadlock was a coalition government. A **coalition** is the joining of different political parties into one government. Together they could do what no one party could do by itself. Brown was saying that he would co-operate with any government to settle the problems of deadlock in Canada, even if it meant co-

John A. Macdonald in 1865

John A. became a favourite subject of political cartoonists. They caricatured his large nose, tall slender body, and curly dark hair.

will be grateful to those who accomplish it.

Brown persuaded many Grits to join with Macdonald and the Tories to break the deadlock. The coalition government had two plans. The first was to try to form a union, or confederation, of all the British colonies in North America. This was not a new idea. William Lyon Mackenzie and Lord Durham had both dreamed of uniting all the British North American colonies under a central government. This plan would give each province its own government to look after local concerns. There would be one central government, based on representation by population, to govern over all the provinces.

If this first plan failed, the alternative was to split Canada again into two provinces (Ontario and Quebec). Each province would run its own local affairs, but there would be a central government based on representation by population to look after matters of concern to both provinces. Other colonies could come in later if they desired. The idea of Confederation was beginning to gain momentum in Canada.

operating with his old enemy, John A. Macdonald! Brown explained why he was prepared to co-operate:

If a crisis has ever arisen in the political affairs of any country that would justify such a coalition, such a crisis has now arrived in the history of Canada....I do say, that if by any means we can find a solution to the difficulties, every man who has the slightest interest in the country

Developing Skills: Cause-and-Effect Relationships

All of the problems you have been reading about can be seen as "causes" of Confederation. A **cause** is the incident that makes something happen. An **effect** is the result or consequence. For example, if your team does not practise, if your star player is hurt, or if luck is not with you, your team may lose the basketball championship. Several causes may lead to the final result—the loss.

At the same time, any event may have several effects. All of the causes and effects together may eventually lead to a major event or change. Suppose a new highrise office building is to be constructed next to your home. What effects might this have? What final change or decision might result? Let's consider the possibilities.

Cause	Effects
A new highrise building is constructed next to your home.	1. Traffic will increase on your street.
	2. The noise level will rise in your neighbourhood.
	3. The highrise will block out the sunlight you receive in the afternoons.
	4. There will be less privacy in your backyard.
	5. The neighbourhood will not be as safe for your little brother to play in because of the increased traffic.
Decision	Your family decides to sell the house and move to a new neighbourhood.

Cause	Effects
1. American Civil War, 1861-1865	1. Britain appears to support the South. This causes resentment among the Northern states.
	2. Northerners stop a British vessel and take two Southerners prisoner. Britain is insulted.
	3. Britain sells armed cruisers to the South. After the war the North demands payment for damages.
	4. Southern soldiers stage raids on Northern states out of Canada. The North is angry at Canada for allowing the raids.
	5. The British North American colonies fear the North may try to get back at Britain by attacking them. They begin to think about uniting to put up a strong defence.
2. American expansionism	
3. Fenian raids	
4. Britain's free trade policy	
5. End of reciprocity with the US	
6. Railway building	
7. Changing British attitude towards colonies	
8. Political deadlock in the Canadas	

Historians examine causes and effects to help understand how and why major events happened. Confederation was a major decision in Canadian history. It had many causes, each with several effects. All of these causes and effects together pushed the colonies to unite.

Using a cause-and-effect organizer can help to understand the complex reasons for Confederation. Consider the example shown here. The first cause listed is the American Civil War. The effects of this war on the British North American colonies are listed to the right. Examine them carefully. Now complete a copy of this organizer in your notebook by filling in the effects of the other events or causes listed. When you have finished, look over all of the causes and effects. Can you see how all of these events together might lead to the major decision that created Canada?

The Charlottetown Conference, 1864

In the summer of 1864, politicians from Nova Scotia, New Brunswick, and Prince Edward Island were planning to meet in Charlottetown to discuss a union of the Maritime colonies. These colonies had been talking about a union for several years. Unexpectedly, they received a request from politicians in Canada asking if they could join the discussions. The

Delegates to the Charlottetown Conference, 1864

Canadians wanted to talk about their plan for an even wider union. The Maritime delegates agreed to hear them out.

On 29 August 1864, the *Queen Victoria* left Quebec City for Charlottetown carrying several important Canadian politicians. Among them were George Brown, John A. Macdonald, George-Étienne Cartier, Alexander Galt, and D'Arcy McGee. They had worked out a plan for a union of all the British North American colonies and hoped to convince the politicians of the Maritime colonies to consider their ideas.

For a week, the Canadians put forward the reasons why the Maritime colonies should join in a union with Canada. The Saint John daily newspaper reported that the arguments of Macdonald, Brown, Cartier, and the other Canadians were "almost irresistible." As they talked, the delegates became convinced that Confederation could work.

The parties and social festivities of the conference also added to the friendly atmosphere. The luncheon on the *Queen Victoria* was arguably the most important piece of shipboard hospitality in Canadian history. Most of the delegates decided that afternoon that Confederation was a real possibility.

As a result of the **Charlottetown Conference**, the Maritime delegates set aside the idea of a Maritime union. They agreed to meet with the Canadians for further discussions at Quebec City in October.

The Quebec Conference, 1864

At Quebec City that October, seven delegates from New Brunswick, seven from Prince Edward Island, and five from Nova Scotia met the twelve delegates from Canada East and Canada West once again. Newfoundland, which had not been represented at Charlottetown, also sent two officials.

At the **Quebec Conference**, the Founders of Confederation agreed on

The Founders of Confederation. This painting combines the delegates to the Charlottetown and Quebec conferences.

one point: the union must be a strong one that could not be broken by any one province. The central government must be more powerful in every way than the governments of the provinces.

But there were other factors to be worked out. How many representatives would each province have in the central government? Where would the money come from to run the central government? What powers would the prime minister have? Would they have two houses of Parliament as the British system had? Would there be an elected House of Commons to make the laws? Would there be an appointed House of Lords to double check the laws passed by the House of Commons? Would other colonies, such as British Columbia, be able to enter Confederation in the future? When these and many other questions had been discussed, the delegates drew up the **Seventy-two Resolutions**. These resolutions provided a plan for the new partnership of the colonies.

During the summer and fall of 1864, the idea of Confederation caught on. Before that time, most of the politicians involved had been strangers to one another. Now they found themselves working together to create a new nation. Yet there were still many hurdles ahead before Confederation would become a reality.

First the Seventy-two Resolutions had to be accepted by the government of each colony. The founders of Confederation went home to convince their people of the idea. Would they be as excited about Confederation as the delegates to the Charlottetown and Quebec conferences were?

The Colonies React

Seesaw in New Brunswick

In New Brunswick, Premier Leonard Tilley was a staunch supporter of Confederation. After the Quebec

Samuel Leonard Tilley

But Leonard Tilley did not give up. In the months that followed, he travelled throughout the colony talking to people and explaining Confederation. His efforts won over many people to the idea.

Three other events helped to convince New Brunswickers that there could be no progress without Confederation. First, the United States ended reciprocity with the British North American colonies. Without free trade, New Brunswick would have to find new trading partners among the other colonies. Second, the British government sent a message encouraging New Brunswickers to join Confederation. Third, the Fenians attacked New Brunswick in 1866. Citizens were terrified as word spread of hundreds of Fenians gathering near the border. While the Fenian threat was still present, an election was called. The people had another chance to say if they wanted Confederation. This time, New Brunswickers listened to Leonard Tilley and voted in favour of Confederation in 1866.

Conference, Tilley called an election in New Brunswick. Confederation was the main issue. Those who were opposed to Confederation **(anti-Confederationists)** argued that, with a population of only 250 000, New Brunswickers would have little influence in any confederation built on the principles of representation by population.

At the Quebec Conference, it had been decided that each province would receive an annual grant, called a **subsidy**, from the central government. The amount of the subsidy was based on the population of the colony. In the case of New Brunswick, the subsidy amounted to 80¢ per person. Anti-Confederationists complained that Tilley was selling New Brunswickers out to the Canadians for 80¢ each!

On election day in 1865, the anti-Confederationists won easily. It was a black day for those who dreamed of a great united country. Without New Brunswick, there could be no Confederation because New Brunswick was the land link between Canada and the other Atlantic colonies.

Success in Canada West

In Canada, the politicians spent more than a month debating the Quebec Conference resolutions. One of the most impressive speeches in the Assembly was given by George Brown. He gave six main reasons why he favoured Confederation:

1. Confederation would change five unimportant colonies into a great and powerful nation.
2. It would remove the barriers to trade among the colonies and provide a market of 4 million people.
3. Canada would become the third largest seafaring nation in the

world, after Britain and the United States.

4. A strong new country would encourage people to come from other countries to settle in Canada.

5. Since the United States had cancelled reciprocity with the colonies, Confederation would provide other markets for their goods.

6. In case of war, all the colonies would stand together to defend each other.

The people of Canada West listened to respected leaders such as George Brown and John A. Macdonald. When the vote was taken in 1865, the Quebec Resolutions were approved by a vote of ninety-one to thirty-three.

About the time of Confederation, George Brown withdrew from politics to devote all his attention to his newspaper, *The Globe*. In 1873, he was appointed to the Senate. Would Confederation have been possible without Brown? He had sacrificed himself and his party to form the coalition government. Certainly his strong leadership helped to bring about Confederation.

Debate in Canada East

In Canada East, there were bitter critics of the plan for Confederation. A.A. Dorion complained that Canada East was being sold out. He argued that French-speaking Canadians would be completely outnumbered in Confederation because the new government would be based on representation by population. The provinces with the largest population would receive the most seats in the legislature.

A majority of French-Canadians were eventually won over to the idea of Confederation by George-Étienne Cartier. For years he and Macdonald had worked together to govern the united province of Canada. Cartier travelled around Canada East trying to persuade French-speaking citizens that they had no reason to worry. He explained that in Confederation French and English Canadians would be equal partners. He promised they would not lose their language, their religion, or their schools. He warned them that if they did not join Confederation, Canada East could be swallowed up by the United States. The Roman Catholic Church also added its voice in support of Confederation.

When it came time to vote in 1865, twenty-six of the forty-eight French-speaking members of the combined Assembly of Canada East and Canada West voted for Confederation. Cartier and the supporters of Confederation had carried the day.

Division in Nova Scotia

Charles Tupper, the premier of Nova Scotia, was excited and enthusiastic about the possibility of a union. But when he returned to Halifax from Quebec, he faced trouble. A powerful

In Nova Scotia, Joseph Howe led the campaign against Confederation

separatist movement had come to life in Nova Scotia. Opposition leaders, especially Joseph Howe, were fiercely opposed to union. They objected to the subsidy, which in Nova Scotia amounted to 40¢ per person. "Tupper has sold out to central Canada for a grant of 40¢ per person—the price of a sheepskin," roared Joseph Howe.

Tupper knew that if he tried to introduce the Seventy-two Resolutions in the Assembly, he would be defeated. Instead, he stalled for time. He travelled throughout the colony trying to destroy the arguments of Howe and the anti-Confederationists. Bitter statements were issued on both sides. The people of Nova Scotia were deeply divided.

About that time, word reached Nova Scotia of the Fenian threat to New Brunswick. Many thought that there was a real possibility Nova Scotia would be invaded too. Nova Scotia would never agree to a union without New Brunswick. But now, with the Fenian threat, New Brunswickers had started to talk seriously about joining Confederation. Some people in Nova Scotia began to hint that they would reconsider if they received a better deal from Ottawa.

Tupper suggested that delegates from the colonies should meet in London, England, to work out a plan that would satisfy them all. While they were there, Howe continued his fight in Nova Scotia, but to no avail. Confederation became a reality and Nova Scotia entered the partnership. Tupper became an important Member of Parliament at Ottawa, and for a short time in 1896 he was prime minister.

Rejection in Newfoundland and Labrador

Newfoundland and Labrador flatly rejected the Quebec Resolutions and waited eighty-two years before joining Canada. The colony had not sent representatives to Charlottetown. However, two delegates had attended the Quebec Conference. One of them, F.B.T. Carter, became the colony's premier in 1865. Although Carter personally was in favour of Confederation, he could not convince his independent people. They were proud of their historic ties with Britain and the fact that they were Britain's first overseas colony.

A wealthy St. John's merchant, C.F. Bennett, led the fight against Confederation. He warned that the new government would probably tax their boats, fish, and fishing tackle. Goods from Canada, he said, would be so cheap that products from Newfoundland and Labrador would not sell. He hinted that young people from the colony would be expected to give up their lives "in defence of the desert sands" of Canada, though Canada had promised that they would not have to serve in the army on the mainland.

On the night Confederation was defeated in Newfoundland in 1866, a huge parade wound through the streets of St. John's. Anti-Confederationists pushed a large coffin labelled "Confederation." The coffin was buried during a mock funeral. Confederation was a dead issue. It stayed buried until 1949 when Newfoundland and Labrador joined Canada as the tenth province.

Rejection in Prince Edward Island

Prince Edward Island also rejected the Quebec Resolutions in 1866. It was not until six years after Confederation, in 1873, that Prince Edward Island entered the union.

Prince Edward Islanders were disappointed that Charlottetown was not chosen as the new capital of Canada. The idea of a union had been born at the Charlottetown Conference and many Islanders thought their city deserved the honour.

Anti-Confederation Song

Hurrah for our own native isle, Newfoundland!
Not a stranger shall hold one inch of its strand!
Her face turns to Britain, her back to the Gulf,
Come near at your peril, Canadian Wolf!

Ye brave Newfoundlanders who plough the salt sea
With hearts like the eagle so bold and so free,
The time is at hand when you'll all have to say
If Confederation will carry the day.

Cheap tea and molasses they say they will give,
All taxes take off that the poor man may live;
Cheap nails and cheap lumber our coffins to make,
And homespun to mend our old clothes when they break.

If they take off the taxes how then will they meet
The heavy expense of the country's upkeep?
Just give them the chance to get us in the scrape
And they'll chain us like slaves with pen, ink, and red tape.

Would you barter the rights that your fathers have won,
Your freedom transmitted from father to son?
For a few thousand dollars of Canadian gold,
Don't let it be said that your birthright was sold.

Then hurrah for our own native isle, Newfoundland!
Not a stranger shall hold one inch of its strand!
Her face turns to Britain, her back to the Gulf,
Come near at your peril, Canadian Wolf!

Edith Fowke, *Folk Songs of Canada* (Waterloo, ON: Waterloo Music Co., 1954).

1. What objections does this song suggest Newfoundlanders had to Confederation?
2. Why is a folk song an effective way to express feelings about key issues? What other folk songs do you know that express strong stands on important issues?
3. Write one other stanza to go before the final refrain in the song or write a stanza for a pro-Confederation song from one of the other colonies.

A more important reason for turning down Confederation was the sheer size of the new country. Prince Edward Islanders feared they would be swamped in the union. The founders had agreed on representation by population in the new parliament. Prince Edward Island had a small population of about 80 00, smaller than the city of Montreal (107 000). With representation by population, Prince Edward Island would have only five members in the House of Commons out of a total of 194. How could the voice of the island be heard with only five members in Parliament?

The people of the island listened to the talk of a railway from Canada to the Maritimes. Since their province was an island, the railway was of no great interest to them. What they needed was a railway to join the places on the island. There was no mention of that in the Quebec Resolutions.

Nor was there any mention of buying out the absentee landlords of the island. Though the Islanders worked the farms, the land was owned by wealthy landlords who lived in Britain. Not until the last minute was it suggested that the new union should buy the land for the Islanders from the landlords for $800 000. But it was too late. The Islanders had made up their minds. They wanted no part of a Confederation in which they had little to gain.

Three founders of Confederation from Prince Edward Island tried to convince their citizens to join. But nothing that John H. Gray, William H. Pope, or Edward Whelan could do or say seemed to make any difference. Prince Edward Island preferred "to stand off and watch the game for a little while."

Confederation Won— The London Conference, 1866

The British North American colonies belonged to Britain. Their union could

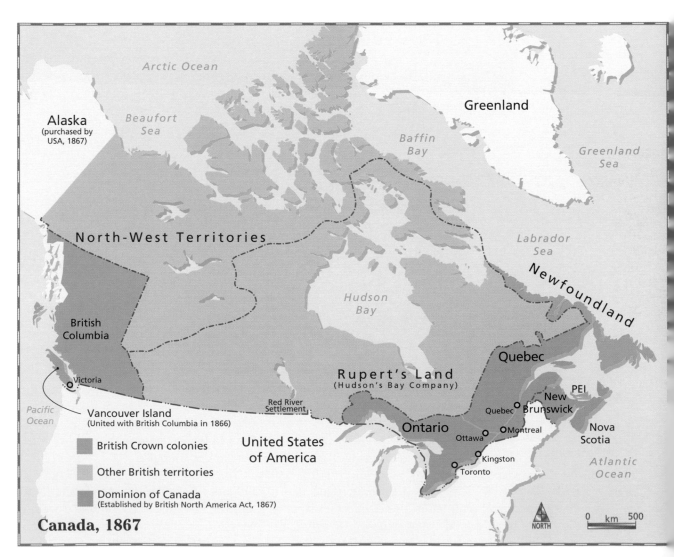

Canada, 1867

Legend:
- British Crown colonies
- Other British territories
- Dominion of Canada (Established by British North America Act, 1867)

Map labels: Arctic Ocean, Alaska (purchased by USA, 1867), Beaufort Sea, Greenland, Baffin Bay, Greenland Sea, North-West Territories, Labrador Sea, Newfoundland, British Columbia, Hudson Bay, Rupert's Land (Hudson's Bay Company), Quebec, Victoria, PEI, New Brunswick, Vancouver Island (United with British Columbia in 1866), Pacific Ocean, Red River Settlement, Quebec, Nova Scotia, Ontario, Montreal, United States of America, Ottawa, Atlantic Ocean, Kingston, Toronto, NORTH, 0 km 500

The London Conference

selves. Many of Britain's responsibilities would be over. In the spring of 1867, the **British North America Act**, often called the **BNA Act**, was introduced in the British Parliament. It united four provinces— New Brunswick, Nova Scotia, and the two Canadas, renamed Ontario and Quebec— as the Dominion of Canada.

not become official until the British Parliament approved it. Therefore sixteen delegates went to discuss the matter in London.

Britain was in favour of Confederation. If the colonies were united, the British hoped they could look after them-

The act was built on the Seventy-two Resolutions worked out at the Quebec Conference. It passed quickly without any major changes. Queen Victoria put her signature on it and 1 July 1867 was proclaimed as the day the act would come into effect.

Dᴇᴠᴇʟᴏᴘɪɴɢ Sᴋɪʟʟs: Iɴᴛᴇʀᴘʀᴇᴛɪɴɢ Pᴏʟɪᴛɪᴄᴀʟ Cᴀʀᴛᴏᴏɴs

The art of political cartoons began early in Canada. Political cartoons were regular features in Canadian newspapers and magazines at the time of Confederation. One of Canada's most noted cartoonists was J.W. Bengough. He made his mark with his caricatures of John A. Macdonald in his weekly magazine *Grip*. **Caricature** involves exaggerating certain characteristics of people to create humour. Through humour, the cartoons made statements about significant issues or events of the day. By poking fun at politics and politicians, cartoonists often helped to put issues into perspective. Cartoons often accompanied the editorials that expressed opinions on key issues.

Political cartoons are still popular today. They appear in newspapers across the country. Leading cartoonists today choose their own subject matter and make their own comments, rather than illustrating the editorials.

Cartoons can be fun to interpret. When you look at political cartoons, ask yourself the following questions:
1. Does the cartoon have a title? If so, what does it mean?
2. What issue or event is referred to in the cartoon?
3. What is the setting? What do you see?
4. Where and when does the action in the cartoon take place?
5. Who are the people or figures in the cartoon? What is their mood? What are they saying?
6. What other objects, symbols, or words are in the cartoon? What do they mean?
7. What comparisons, if any, are being made?
8. At whom or what is the cartoonist poking fun?
9. What is the message of the cartoon?
10. Does the cartoonist get the message across effectively? Why or why not?

11. How does the cartoonist create humour? What techniques are used to get the message across?

12. Does the cartoonist's viewpoint differ from yours? In what way?

Try It!

1. Now you can try to interpret a political cartoon yourself. This cartoon by J.W. Bengough appeared at the time of Confederation. He is examining the question, Who is the founder of Confederation? Several politicians are shown, including John A. Macdonald, George Brown, and William McDougall. Using the questions above, interpret this cartoon.

2. Clip modern political cartoons from your local newspaper. Use the same questions to interpret these cartoons. Discuss similarities and differences between modern cartoons and those from the last century.

CONFEDERATION!

THE MUCH-FATHERED YOUNGSTER.

Celebration!

On 1 July 1867, most of the people in the new country of Canada took a holiday. In Toronto, a great celebration took place at the Horticultural Gardens. The gardens were lighted with Chinese lanterns. Fresh strawberries and ice cream were served. A concert was followed by dancing. In Quebec, boat races on the St. Lawrence River, horse races, and cricket matches were held. In Atlantic Canada, many families travelled to the sea for a day of swim-ming and a picnic supper of salads, cold meat, pies, and cakes. Almost everywhere, there was the feeling that this day was just the beginning of great things for Canada.

But in some parts of the new Dominion the mood was not one of rejoicing. Anti-Confederationists displayed flags at half-mast. They wore black clothes as a sign of mourning. A likeness of Dr. Tupper was burned side-by-side with a rat in Nova Scotia. In New Brunswick, a newspaper carried a death notice on its front page: "Died—at her residence in the city of Fredericton, The Province of New Brunswick, in the eighty-third year of her age."

Models for Government

Before Confederation, the British North American colonies had responsible government. Members were elected by the people to a Legislative Assembly. Executive and legislative councils were chosen from the party with the most members in the Assembly. The governor was the representative of the queen or king of Britain and the head of the colonial government. He was required, however, to follow the advice of the councillors and the Assembly. The founders of Confederation kept responsible government, but the organization of government changed.

In forming the new government for Canada, the founders of Confederation had two models: the British and the American. They selected what they believed were the best features of both.

The British Model

Canada was still loyal to Britain, so the queen would continue to be the head of state for the Canadian government. There was no talk of separation from Britain. A Governor-General would be the queen's representative in Canada.

It was also decided that Canada would have a **parliamentary government** fashioned on the example of the British system. The British government had a prime minister and a cabinet of senior ministers who controlled government policy. They were all members of the political party that had the most representatives in the House of Commons.

The House of Commons was made up of representatives elected by the people. The government would be responsible to the people of Canada. If the prime minis-

ter and his party lost the support of a majority of the members in the House of Commons, they could be voted out of power.

In Canada, the House of Commons would consist of elected representatives from each of the provinces. Quebec was guaranteed sixty-five members to ensure a strong voice for the French-speaking population. The other provinces would elect members on the basis of their populations.

The British government also had a second house of Parliament called the House of Lords. Canada would also have a second house, but it would be called the Senate. The name was taken from the American system. There were to be seventy-two lifetime members in the Senate—twenty-four from Quebec, twenty-four from Ontario, and twenty-four from the Maritimes. The main function of the Senate was to double check all laws passed by the elected House of Commons.

With responsible government, the executive and legislative councils were chosen from the party with the most members in the elected Assembly. They were responsible to the people and the governor was obliged to follow their advice. At Confederation, the real power for governing the country and making laws went to the prime minister and cabinet, who represented the party with the majority in the elected House of Commons.

The American Model

From the American system of government, Canadians chose the idea of a **federal union**. In a federal union, a federal or central government deals with matters of concern to the whole nation. But each province or state deals with its own affairs independently of the central government. In other words, the Canadian provinces could make their own deci-

The development of government

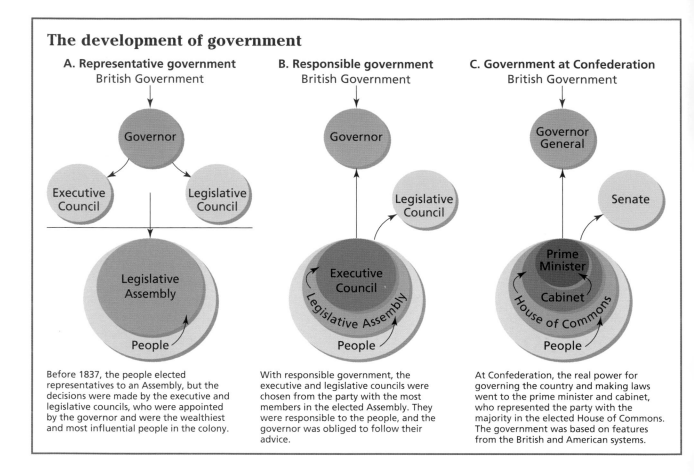

A. Representative government
British Government

Governor

Executive Council

Legislative Council

Legislative Assembly

People

Before 1837, the people elected representatives to an Assembly, but the decisions were made by the executive and legislative councils, who were appointed by the governor and were the wealthiest and most influential people in the colony.

B. Responsible government
British Government

Governor

Legislative Council

Executive Council

Legislative Assembly

People

With responsible government, the executive and legislative councils were chosen from the party with the most members in the elected Assembly. They were responsible to the people, and the governor was obliged to follow their advice.

C. Government at Confederation
British Government

Governor General

Senate

Prime Minister

Cabinet

House of Commons

People

At Confederation, the real power for governing the country and making laws went to the prime minister and cabinet, who represented the party with the majority in the elected House of Commons. The government was based on features from the British and American systems.

sions on roads, for example, without having to ask permission from the federal government.

The questions then arose: What powers should the federal government have? What powers should the provincial governments have? Here again, the founders of Confederation learned from the American example.

In their federation, the Americans gave broad powers to the states, with limited powers to the central government. Macdonald thought this was the great weakness of the American system. The Civil War that had just ended arose out of a dispute over the rights of individual states. Macdonald wanted to avoid this mistake in Canada at all costs. Therefore he saw Canada with a strong central government and less powerful provincial governments.

The Division of Powers

The founders of Confederation purposely set out to give as little power to the provinces as possible. Provinces were responsible for education, the ownership of the land and natural resources, property rights, mines and forests, business licences, provincial taxes, and other matters of provincial concern. All other powers belonged to the federal government. John A. Macdonald said in 1864:

In framing the Constitution, care should be taken to avoid the mistakes and weaknesses of the United States system. Their primary error was reserving for the states all powers not given to the central government. We must reverse this....A strong central government is essential to the success of the experiment we are trying.

The federal government would control trade, defence, foreign affairs, banks, shipping, fisheries, and criminal law. It was also given the power to tax the people. In addition, the federal government could disallow any law passed by the provinces. The British North America Act declared that "Indians and lands reserved for Indians" were the responsibility of the federal government. This is the only mention of aboriginal peoples in the act.

Finances

By the BNA Act, the federal government took over all the debts of the provinces. It also took over most of the provinces' sources of income, such as customs duties. Every province was given a sum of money, or **subsidy,** by the federal government each year. The amount of money was based on the province's population.

Other Matters

The British North America Act promised that an intercolonial railway connecting the St. Lawrence River with Halifax would be started within six months. It also allowed for other provinces to join the Dominion in the future.

The founders of Confederation were careful to protect the rights of the French-speaking people of Quebec. French-Canadians could keep their own province, language, religion, and schools. Both Roman Catholic and Protestant schools were guaranteed. English and French languages were to be used in the central Parliament, in the Parliament of Quebec, and in the federal courts. Thus the new country of Canada was firmly established.

CONFEDERATION UPDATE: TIMELINE OF CONFEDERATION SINCE 1867

Nellie McClung (left) campaigned for women's right to vote

Canada today is not the Canada of 1867. Democratic governments always grow and change. The following timeline outlines how Canadian Confederation has changed since 1867.

1869	Canada purchases Hudson's Bay Company lands
1870	Manitoba enters Confederation
1871	British Columbia enters Confederation
1873	Prince Edward Island enters Confederation
1876	The Indian Act is passed
1905	Alberta becomes a province
1905	Saskatchewan becomes a province
1912	Manitoba, Ontario, and Quebec are enlarged to their present boundaries
1916	Manitoba is the first province to grant women the right to vote
1918	All women in Canada receive the right to vote in federal elections
1931	The Statute of Westminster serves as Britain's official recognition of Canada's complete control over its own affairs. Until this time, some important decisions, such as international treaties, were still being made in Britain
1947	Chinese-Canadians receive the right to vote

1948	Citizens of Japanese descent receive the right to vote in federal elections
1949	Citizens of Japanese descent receive the right to vote in provincial elections in British Columbia
1949	Newfoundland joins Confederation
1960	Status Indians, or registered Indians, are granted the right to vote in federal elections
1964	Canada adopts a new flag—a single red maple leaf with red bars on a white background
1967	Canadians celebrate Canada's 100th birthday. To mark the event, schools, libraries, concert halls, stadiums, and skating rinks are built in cities, towns, and villages across the country. The world is invited to help all Canadians celebrate at the world's fair, Expo '67, in Montreal
1969	The **Official Languages Act** is passed, making French and English the official languages of Canada. The act ensures that Canadians can be served by the federal government in French and English
1970	The legal voting age for federal elections is lowered to eighteen
1971	The federal government supports multiculturalism. It encourages Canadians to take pride in the customs and traditions of varied ethnic backgrounds
1980	Quebec votes "No" to sovereignty association
1980	Parliament recognizes "O Canada" as the national anthem
1982	The **Constitution Act** creates the Canadian Charter of Rights and Freedoms and a mechanism for amending the Constitution
1984	The Young Offenders Act gives young people between twelve and seventeen years full legal rights in the criminal justice system
1984	Jeanne Sauvé becomes the first female Governor-General of Canada
1985	The government amends the Indian Act so that Indian women who lost their Indian status through marriage can regain it
1987	The House of Commons approves the **Meech Lake Accord**, a constitutional amendment that recognizes Quebec as a distinct society. The agreement fails to pass in the legislatures of Manitoba and Newfoundland
1989	The Free Trade Agreement between Canada and the United States comes into effect
1991	An agreement is reached on Nunavut, a new northern territory
1992	The **Charlottetown Accord** is hammered out by Prime Minister Brian Mulroney and the provincial premiers. It proposes constitutional amendments that would recognize Quebec as a distinct soci-

Canada Day celebrations

Multicultural celebrations

ety and sets the groundwork for aboriginal self-government and a reformed Senate, along with other proposals

1992   In a national referendum, the Charlottetown Accord is rejected by the people of Canada

1994   The North American Free Trade Agreement is signed

1995   The sovereignty referendum in Quebec is narrowly defeated

The federalist rally in Montreal, 1995

Activities

Check Your Understanding

1. Add the following terms to your *Factfile* on Canadian history:

   • Confederation • American Civil War • Manifest Destiny • Fenians • Reciprocity Treaty, 1854 • Grand Trunk Railway • Little Englanders • Charlottetown Conference, 1864 • Quebec Conference, 1864 • Seventy-two Resolutions • anti-Confederationists • British North America Act (BNA Act) • parliamentary system • federal union.

2. Why were the British North American colonies concerned about an American invasion in 1865?

3. a) Who were the Fenians and what were their goals?
   b) How did they try to achieve these goals?
   c) In which British North American colonies did the Fenians have the greatest effect on public opinion? Why?
   d) How did the Fenians help the cause of Confederation?

4. a) Who were the Little Englanders? What were their main beliefs?
   b) Why did they cause Canadians to worry?

5. a) What problems with trade were the colonies facing in the 1860s? How did these problems provide a push for Confederation?
   b) Why were more railway links important?

6. What major decisions were made at:
   a) the Charlottetown Conference
   b) the Quebec Conference
   c) the London Conference?

7. Which colonies approved the Seventy-two Resolutions? Which rejected them?

Confirm Your Learning

8. Create a mind map to record the problems that were pushing the British North American colonies together during the 1860s.

9. George-Étienne Cartier said: "When all colonies are united the enemy will know that if he attacks any province he will have to deal with the combined forces of the Empire."
   a) Who was "the enemy"?
   b) Who were "the combined forces of the Empire"?
   c) Why were British troops stationed in the colonies?
   d) Why would it be difficult for an individual colony to defend itself?

10. In groups, summarize the common problems that moved the colonies towards union. Rank these in order of importance and discuss the reasons for your ranking.

11. What arguments might each of the following give for preferring a Maritime union rather than a union of all the colonies? Explain your answers.
    a) a Nova Scotia merchant
    b) a Prince Edward Island farmer
    c) a New Brunswick railway worker
    d) a Newfoundlander who earns a living from fishing.

12. a) Why did the people of Newfoundland and Prince Edward Island reject Confederation?
    b) Outline reasons why the Canadas, New Brunswick, and Nova Scotia supported the union of the colonies.

13. a) The BNA Act set out the powers of the federal and provincial governments. Create a two- column organizer with the headings "Federal Powers" and "Provincial Powers." Place the items in the following list in the correct columns.
    - defence
    - education
    - mines and forests
    - fisheries
    - customs duties
    - criminal law
    - property rights
    - banks
    - taxation
    - licensing of businesses
    - immigration
    - trade
    - foreign affairs
    - aboriginal affairs

    b) Which government received the greatest powers? Why?
    c) Do you agree this division of powers was a good one? Explain.

14. a) On what kind of union did the founders of Confederation decide? Why?
    b) How was it different from the American one? Why?

15. *Extra! Extra! Read all about it!* Write newspaper headlines reflecting the mood and events in each of the colonies after the Confederation votes.

16. Based on your study of Confederation, do you think the founders of Confederation intended that any province should leave the union? Explain your answer. Why might provinces such as British Columbia, Nova Scotia, or Quebec choose to leave Canada? If one or more provinces left the union, would the rest of Canada break up? What do you think would happen?

Challenge Your Mind

17. a) What are the advantages and disadvantages for Canada of reciprocity with the United States?

    b) Does Canada have reciprocity with the United States today? Do the provinces have reciprocity with each other today?

18. Suppose you are a political cartoonist for a newspaper in New Brunswick, Nova Scotia, Prince Edward Island, or Newfoundland. Draw an anti-Confederation cartoon for your paper.

19. The aboriginal peoples of British North America were not consulted about Confederation. They were not given a chance to decide whether or not it would be good for them or how they might be part of it. How do you think they felt? How might Canada be different today if aboriginal peoples had been able to express their point of view?

20. If your town or city is older than Confederation, try to find out how the birth of Confederation was celebrated (or mourned). Local libraries and old newspapers will help you. Create a mural depicting the event.

21. Some French-speaking students from Quebec were talking with some English-speaking students from the Prairies. They said to each other: "We don't know you! You don't know us!" What do you think the students meant by this remark? Is it true? How much do you know about other regions of Canada and the people in them? Why is it important for Confederation that Canadians understand how other Canadians feel and think?

CHAPTER 3

Exploring and Opening the West

ABORIGINAL PEOPLES: THE FIRST CANADIANS

The first people to make North America their permanent home were aboriginal peoples. By the time Europeans arrived in the sixteenth century, aboriginal peoples had been in Canada for 10 000 years. They had developed their own distinct cultures. **Culture** is the way of life of a group of

The SS Beaver *off Fort Victoria, 1846*

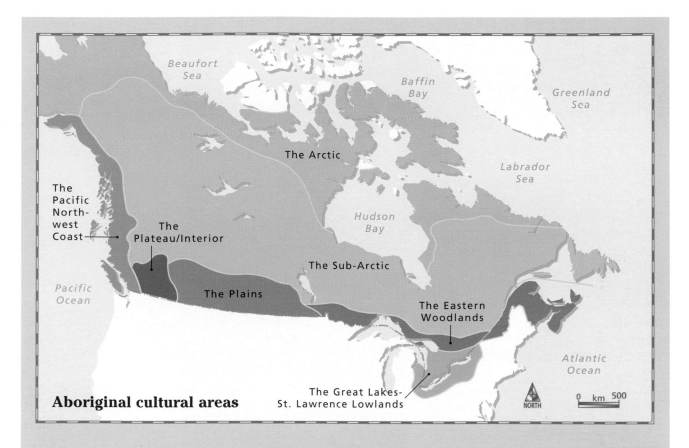

Beaufort
Sea

Baffin
Bay

Greenland
Sea

The Arctic

Labrador
Sea

The
Pacific
North-
west
Coast

The
Plateau/Interior

Hudson
Bay

Pacific
Ocean

The Sub-Arctic

The Plains

The Eastern
Woodlands

Atlantic
Ocean

Aboriginal cultural areas

The Great Lakes-
St. Lawrence Lowlands

NORTH

0   km   500

people. It includes everything about the way the people live—homes, clothing, artifacts, daily routines, and seasonal activities, as well as their ideas and beliefs. The culture of Canada's aboriginal peoples was largely influenced by the environment in which they lived. The people learned to use the resources around them without harming the environment.

The aboriginal peoples of Canada were roughly divided into seven cultural areas before the arrival of the Europeans: the Pacific Northwest Coast, the Plateau/Interior, the Plains, the Sub-Arctic, the Arctic, the Eastern Woodlands, and the Great Lakes-St. Lawrence Lowlands. Four of the seven cultural areas— the Pacific Northwest Coast, the Plains, the Plateau/Interior, and the Sub-Arctic—are found in what are today British Columbia and the prairie provinces. In this chapter you will look at these four cultural areas to discover how the environment influenced the culture of the aboriginal peoples who lived there.

Aboriginal Cultural Areas

Location and Landscape

Pacific Northwest Coast

The people of the cultural area of the Pacific Northwest Coast lived in villages along a narrow strip of coastline from northern California to the panhandle of Alaska. The area was bordered by snow-capped mountains on the east. On the west, along the Pacific Ocean, was a jagged coastline of countless inlets and steep-sided fiords, which cut long, narrow, and extremely deep channels into the shore. There was a wide, offshore band consisting of numerous islands. The largest of these was Vancouver Island, at approximately 32 500 km^2. Other islands were little more than rocky outcrops. Because the aboriginal peoples were coastal dwellers, the water, tides, and weather were decisive influences on their lifestyle.

The Plains

The cultural area of the Plains stretched from central Saskatchewan and Alberta

Giant trees and thick underbrush were common features of the Pacific Northwest Coast environment.

Grass was the main vegetation on the dry landscape of the Plains.

in Canada to the south-central United States. Made up almost entirely of dry prairie grasslands, the land was flat to gently rolling and predominantly treeless. The prairie, however, was pockmarked by many tree-fringed sloughs, salt-encrusted potholes, and low sandy hills. Only a few rivers flowed through the area, and they provided almost all of the available water.

Not all of Canada between the Great Lakes and the Rocky Mountains was prairie. There was an area of parkland of alternating forest and open clearings covered with high grasses. It extended west from the Red River to the north branch of the Saskatchewan and into the Peace River country of modern British Columbia.

The Plateau/Interior

From the Yukon in the north to the United States-Canada border, there was a great valley between the Coast Range and the Rocky Mountains. From north to south it stretched over 1300 km and varied from 240 km to 320 km in width. Across such a huge area, the landscape varied considerably. In the north there were high mountains and dense forests. Further south, between Prince Rupert and Prince George, stretched lakes, mountains, and forests. Still further south, the country became increasingly drier. Several rivers drained through the area, cutting deep valleys called canyons or gorges.

The Sub-Arctic

The cultural area of the Sub-Arctic stretched all the way across North America from Alaska in the west to Newfoundland in the east. It was an enormous area that took up over 25 percent of all of Canada. This area was dotted with thousands of little lakes, and several very large ones, including Great Bear Lake and Great Slave Lake. It was also crossed by hundreds of rivers. A vast coniferous (evergreen) forest, mostly spruce, was the main vegetation. As the land got higher or stretched further north, the forest thinned out and gave way to open tundra covered with dense mats of mosses and lichens. Much of the region was empty as there were many parts where the game was so scarce that the people could not obtain enough food to live on.

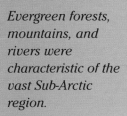

The landscape of the Plateau was rugged and varied. The southern region, shown in this photograph, was generally dry with few trees.

Evergreen forests, mountains, and rivers were characteristic of the vast Sub-Arctic region.

A woman's saddle, decorated with beadwork, from the Blackfoot society

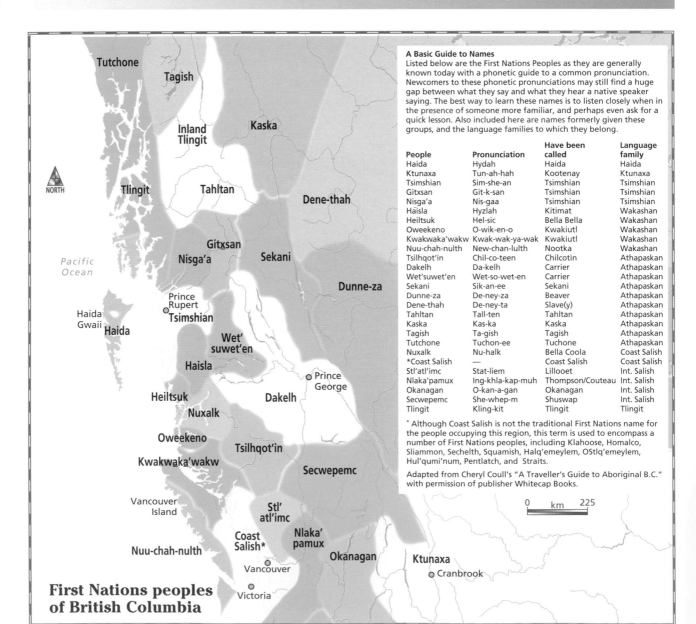

A Basic Guide to Names

Listed below are the First Nations Peoples as they are generally known today with a phonetic guide to a common pronunciation. Newcomers to these phonetic pronunciations may still find a huge gap between what they say and what they hear a native speaker saying. The best way to learn these names is to listen closely when in the presence of someone more familiar, and perhaps even ask for a quick lesson. Also included here are names formerly given these groups, and the language families to which they belong.

People	Pronunciation	Have been called	Language family
Haida	Hydah	Haida	Haida
Ktunaxa	Tun-ah-hah	Kootenay	Ktunaxa
Tsimshian	Sim-she-an	Tsimshian	Tsimshian
Gitxsan	Git-k-san	Tsimshian	Tsimshian
Nisga'a	Nis-gaa	Tsimshian	Tsimshian
Haisla	Hyzlah	Kitimat	Wakashan
Heiltsuk	Hel-sic	Bella Bella	Wakashan
Oweekeno	O-wik-en-o	Kwakiutl	Wakashan
Kwakwaka'wakw	Kwak-wak-ya-wak	Kwakiutl	Wakashan
Nuu-chah-nulth	New-chan-lulth	Nootka	Wakashan
Tsilhqot'in	Chil-co-teen	Chilcotin	Athapaskan
Dakelh	Da-kelh	Carrier	Athapaskan
Wet'suwet'en	Wet-so-wet-en	Carrier	Athapaskan
Sekani	Sik-an-ee	Sekani	Athapaskan
Dunne-za	De-ney-za	Beaver	Athapaskan
Dene-thah	De-ney-ta	Slave(y)	Athapaskan
Tahltan	Tall-ten	Tahltan	Athapaskan
Kaska	Kas-ka	Kaska	Athapaskan
Tagish	Ta-gish	Tagish	Athapaskan
Tutchone	Tuchon-ee	Tuchone	Athapaskan
Nuxalk	Nu-halk	Bella Coola	Coast Salish
*Coast Salish	—	Coast Salish	Coast Salish
Stl'atl'imc	Stat-liem	Lillooet	Int. Salish
Nlaka'pamux	Ing-khla-kap-muh	Thompson/Couteau	Int. Salish
Okanagan	O-kan-a-gan	Okanagan	Int. Salish
Secwepemc	She-whep-m	Shuswap	Int. Salish
Tlingit	Kling-kit	Tlingit	Tlingit

* Although Coast Salish is not the traditional First Nations name for the people occupying this region, this term is used to encompass a number of First Nations peoples, including Klahoose, Homalco, Sliammon, Sechelth, Squamish, Halq'emeylem, OStlq'emeylem, Hul'qumi'num, Pentlatch, and Straits.

Adapted from Cheryl Coull's "A Traveller's Guide to Aboriginal B.C." with permission of publisher Whitecap Books.

0   km   225

First Nations peoples of British Columbia

Map labels: Tutchone, Tagish, Inland Tlingit, Kaska, Tlingit, Tahltan, Dene-thah, Gitxsan, Nisga'a, Sekani, Dunne-za, Pacific Ocean, Prince Rupert, Tsimshian, Haida Gwaii, Haida, Wet'suwet'en, Haisla, Prince George, Heiltsuk, Dakelh, Nuxalk, Oweekeno, Tsilhqot'in, Kwakwaka'wakw, Secwepemc, Vancouver Island, Stl'atl'imc, Nlaka'pamux, Coast Salish*, Okanagan, Ktunaxa, Nuu-chah-nulth, Vancouver, Cranbrook, Victoria, NORTH

Aboriginal Peoples of the Plains and Sub-Arctic

The Plains
Blackfoot
Blood
Peigan
Sarcee
Assiniboine
Gros Ventre
Plains Cree

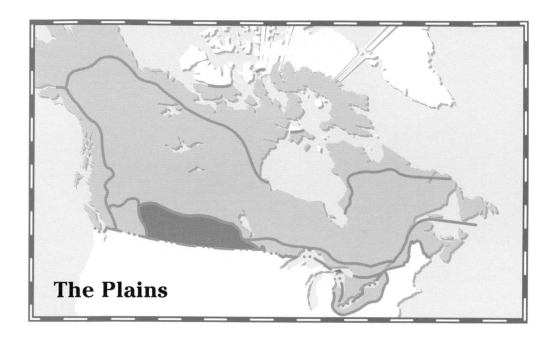

The Sub-Arctic
Chipewyan
Dunne-za
Dene-thah
Cree
Dogrib

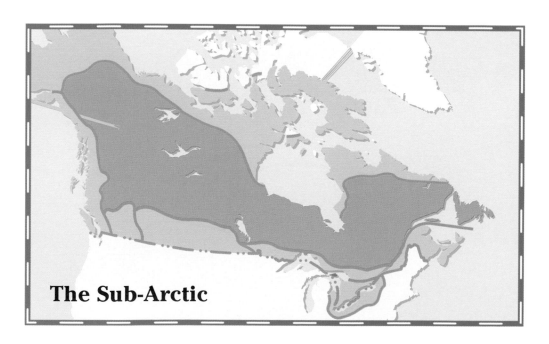

Interior of a plank house, from a painting by Emily Carr

Ktunaxa Sun Dance pole raising

Gloves from the Dene-thah of the Sub-Arctic

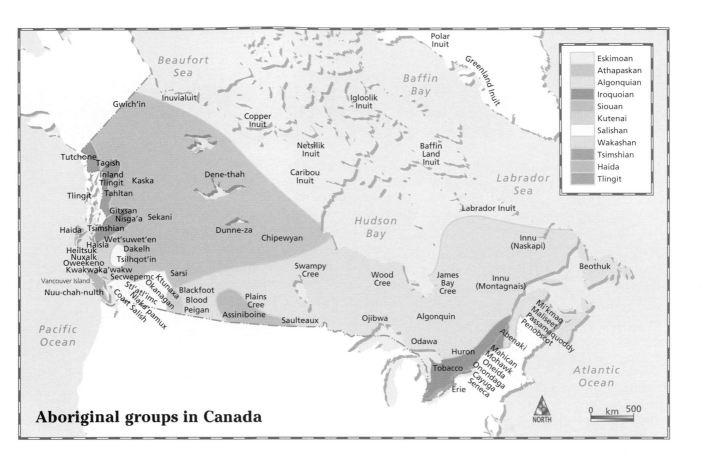

Aboriginal groups in Canada

Climate

Pacific Northwest Coast

The climate of the coastal area was moderated by the Pacific Ocean. This area was blessed with some of the mildest winter temperatures in Canada. Summers were cool. Precipitation along the coast was high due to the barriers created by the mountains. Rain clouds and fog rolled in from the Pacific and nurtured a lush green rainforest with a thick underbrush. Abundant rainfall, mild temperatures, and fertile soil produced colossal red cedar and fir trees, some 1000 years old and almost 100 m high. Hugh cedars provided the people with logs to make canoes and house planks and with flexible bark for "barkcloth" garments. Mountainsides were covered with fir and spruce. The Pacific Northwest Coast culture was distinguished by its imaginative use of wood for buildings, boats, and utensils. Winter brought fierce storms from the sea, with huge waves that battered the shore. In winter, people tended to congregate in their villages and live on food stored in other seasons. It was during the winter, though, that the people of the Northwest occupied themselves with dances, feasts, and potlatches (a status-affirming ceremony involving gift-giving of food, clothing, and tools), and other ceremonial events.

The Plains

The climate in this cultural area was remarkable for its variations. Summers were hot and dry. The aboriginal peoples lived and hunted on open plains during this season. The winters were bitterly cold, with severe winds and blizzards. Aboriginal groups often divided into smaller family groups. They left the open plains and sought protection in the foothills or the river valleys to escape the severe winter conditions.

The Plateau/Interior

The weather was much harsher in this region than on the coast. Summers were generally hot and dry, while winters were extremely cold. The northern region, with its high mountains and dense forests, received more rainfall than the south. The south was much drier as the prevailing winds from the Pacific lost their moisture on the windward side of the Rockies. In the south, the British Columbia Dry Belt contained a semidesert complete with cacti and rattlesnakes. The harshness of the climate meant that it took greater efforts to find food.

The Sub-Arctic

Long harsh winters dominated this cultural area. Temperatures in winter often dipped below -50°C. However, dense forests provided fuel and shelter from the wind for the people. Summers were short and mild with long days and hours of sunlight. Although there were lots of flowers and birds during the summer, plagues of mosquitoes posed a problem. The harsh environment of the Sub-Arctic made life more difficult here than in any other cultural area. However, the aboriginal peoples were able to adapt to their environment.

Food Resources

Pacific Northwest Coast

The range of foodstuffs from the sea was large. Salmon was a mainstay, preserved by smoking over housefires. Candlefish was used for oil and halibut and cod also contributed to the diet. Shellfish were plentiful along the coast and were an important source of food. So many shellfish were eaten that along the coast today you can still see mounds of discarded shells that have piled up over the centuries. Some communities hunted seals, sea lions, and sea otters for food, and the Nuu-chah-nulth (Nootka) pursued and harpooned whales far out at sea. In the dense forests there were moose, deer, elk, caribou, bear, and mountain goats to add to the diet. Land resources, however, were less important than food from the sea.

The Plains

Antelope, elk, and deer lived in this region, but the most important animal was the buffalo. The plains people lived from the buffalo as the Pacific Northwest Coast people lived from the salmon. Vast herds of buffalo, estimated between 50 and 60 million across North America, roamed the plains feeding on the prairie grasses. Because of this migration, trees had little chance of taking hold, and so

A fishing weir. The Haida and other Pacific Northwest Coast peoples used weirs like this one to trap salmon as they swam upstream.

An illustration of buffalo stampeding over the cliffs at Head-Smashed-In Buffalo Jump.

the grasslands spread. Aboriginal peoples gathered on the plains each summer to hunt the buffalo co-operatively. (Hunting was on foot because horses did not reach the Canadian plains until the mid-1700s.) Depending on the landscape, aboriginal peoples stampeded the animals over the edge of cliffs or drove them into **pounds**, or corrals. The greatest number of jump sites have been found in the foothills of the Rocky Mountains. Corrals were more commonly used on the prairies in present-day Saskatchewan and Alberta. Both forms of hunting called for a high degree of co-operation and organization. Not only was buffalo meat important for food, but the hides were used for tipi coverings, shields, and moccasins. The sinew was used for the thread and the bones were fashioned into tools. Buffalo bone marrow and fat were used in the making of **pemmican**—a highly nutritious mixture of berries and dried meat that could last for months without spoiling. Even the dried dung of the buffalo was used as a fuel for the fires.

Lynx are among the small game of the Plateau/Interior

Caribou and other big game roam the Sub-Arctic

The Plateau/Interior

This area was home to big game animals such as the white-tailed deer, caribou, black bear, grizzly bear, elk, and mountain sheep. Coyote, fox, lynx, and beaver were also found in the area. All of the Interior people hunted, even during the snowy winters. They used spears or bows and arrows to kill large animals or snares made of rope to catch smaller game. Some groups lived beside rivers where they could catch the salmon as they came upstream to spawn. Other groups spent the summer near lakes and streams where they could fish for whitefish, suckers, and pike. Vegetable foods consisted mainly of edible roots and a variety of berries. These were dried for winter use. Meat and fish were dried or smoked to preserve them.

The Sub-Arctic

The most important big game animals for hunters were caribou, moose, and black bears. The Sub-Arctic people depended on the caribou in much the same way the people of the plains based their economy on the buffalo. They also hunted smaller woodland animals such as rabbits, beavers, and groundhogs. The many streams, rivers, and lakes of the Sub-Arctic teemed with trout, whitefish, pickerel, and pike. Waterfowl, such as ducks and geese, that passed through the Sub-Arctic in their annual migration were hunted as well. Vegetable foods were mainly berries and the tender shoots of young plants.

Adaptation to the Environment

Pacific Northwest Coast

The aboriginal peoples of the Pacific Northwest Coast adapted well to their environment, living on the wealth supplied by the ocean and rainforest. One of the greatest gifts of the coastal environment, the giant red cedar, provided wood for the world's largest dugout canoes. The canoes allowed the people to harvest the water resources of the coastline. Virtually all travel and communication was by water. Canoes permitted the people to travel along the coast and to reach areas that would have been otherwise inaccessible. Canoes were vital for transportation, trade, work, and warfare. The abundance of fish, especially salmon, meant that there was no need to travel over great distances in search of food. People could live year-round in the same general location. The abundant and readily available resources allowed the coastal area to be densely populated. Before the arrival of the Europeans, the Northwest coast people may have numbered as many as 200 000.

Cedar timbers and planks were used to build large houses in which a number of people, usually family groups, lived under one roof. The houses became the basic social unit in all coastal societies. From the giant cedars the coastal people carved the huge carved totem poles that honoured their guardian spirits.

The Plains

The lifestyle of the Plains people revolved around the changing seasons and the buffalo herds. Plains people did not have permanent villages, but were **nomadic**, travelling from place to place, following the buffalo and other resources. Often in the summer, smaller family hunting groups joined together in large hunting camps. The buffalo hunt required planning, co-operation, and leadership. In summer, people also travelled to areas in search of plant food. Life for the people of the plains was difficult. But they were efficient hunters and gatherers, and they adapted to the changing seasons. Their skills and knowledge of the environment enabled them to live comfortably, except when droughts or floods made animals scarce. Before the arrival of the Europeans, the population of the plains is estimated to have averaged less than one person for every 26 km^2.

The Plateau/Interior

Because the environment was harsher in the interior than on the coast, it took

An aboriginal fishing village on the Pacific Northwest Coast

A Blackfoot family with a travois. What is being carried on this travois?

A Ktunaxa community on the Plateau

A diorama depicting the lifestyle of the Sekani

more effort to find food. Food had to be gathered over vast territories. The people were nomadic. They travelled in small family hunting groups during the spring, summer, and fall. The principal weapons were bows and arrows, clubs, spears, and knives. Traps, snares, and pits dug in the ground were also used. A variety of methods were used for catching fish, including nets, weirs, spears, and ice fishing. In the winter, larger groups gathered together in settled villages. In the south, they lived in circular underground houses called pit houses, which provided insulation from the cold. These houses were protected by cone-shaped roofs made of poles covered with brush and earth. An entrance was left at the top, with a notched log ladder for climbing in and out. In the north, people built log or pole huts with gabled roofs. These had a door at the end and a fire in the middle. In the summer, the aboriginal peoples moved into cone-shaped tents, which were a framework of poles covered with rush mats. These could be taken down easily and moved from place to place.

The Sub-Arctic

Because of the harsh environment, the aboriginal peoples of the Sub-Arctic travelled throughout the year to secure their food supply. They lived in groups of one or two families that worked and travelled together. Although food supplies were often irregular, the people were skilled at surviving in the forests. Because they were nomadic, the people did not require permanent villages. Their homes were made of hides that could be packed up and carried from one place to another. The people often used snares made of rawhide. These were so strong that not even a moose or grizzly bear could break through them. In the west, they built hunting fences that stretched through the forest. Cariboo and moose were snared as they tried to find a way through the fence. Cariboo were often speared in the water from canoes as the herd crossed a river. Fish were caught in nets, with hooks and lines, and with spears. In a region where people could hunt for days and find nothing, they built caches. A **cache** is a French word meaning "hiding place." Surplus food was stored or hidden in the caches.

Early Contact between Aboriginal Peoples and Europeans

Before European settlers came to North America, aboriginal peoples controlled their own lives. They had adapted to their environment by hunting, fishing, or growing their own food. They ran their own governments, educated their children in their own way, and practised their own religions and beliefs. Then one day strangers appeared in their lands.

The strangers came from distant parts of Europe and had their own way of life. They had a different culture, and to the aboriginal peoples who first met them, they must have appeared very strange indeed. The clothing they wore, the vessels they travelled in, and the tools and utensils they carried were totally new to the aboriginal peoples.

Most of the first meetings between the Europeans and aboriginal peoples were friendly. The newcomers were welcomed, and without the help of the aboriginal peoples, the Europeans would have had great difficulty surviving those first years in the unfamiliar and harsh environment. During this early period of contact Europeans and aboriginal peoples traded with each other. The Europeans were eager to obtain furs; in return, the aboriginal peoples bargained for metal knives, copper kettles, guns, and steel traps. They quickly learned the usefulness of these foreign goods.

Gradually, contact between these two different peoples changed the ways of life for both. Some of these changes were positive. The Europeans, for example, learned how to adapt to the Canadian environment. They also adopted many aboriginal inventions, such as the birch-bark canoe and the snowshoe. Aboriginal peoples discovered that the new European tools, weapons, clothes, and food could be incorporated into their culture. With these new things they were able to have greater ease in their daily lives and greater variety in their goods.

Not all of the changes that contact brought were positive for aboriginal peoples, however. As they became more involved in the fur trade, they came to depend on the goods they could obtain from the Europeans. Gradually, some of the traditional aboriginal ways were forgotten. Skills were neglected, and sometimes lost completely. Many aboriginal people also fell victim to European diseases, such as smallpox and measles. So many people died that the aboriginal population was drastically reduced. In the early 1600s, Membertou, a Mi'kmaq at Port Royal, remembered back to the days when the strangers first came to his shore. "In my youth," Membertou said, "I saw my people as thickly planted here as the hairs on my head. Since the French mingled with us, we are dying fast." Changes also took place in the values and beliefs of aboriginal peoples. Believing that their religion was the only true one, European missionaries tried to convert aboriginal peoples to Christianity.

DEVELOPING SKILLS: INTERVIEWING

An interview is a face-to-face meeting between people to talk about a topic or issue. Usually one or both parties wants to obtain information. When you go for an interview for a summer job, you want to know about the job and whether you have the skills to do it. The employer wants to know whether you are the right person for the job.

Journalists make their living conducting interviews. Barry Broadfoot is a newspaper reporter and social historian who collects information through interviews. He travels across Canada talking to people about their experiences. The interviews are collected in books describing Canadian life during the Great Depression and the Second World War. Books and interviews like these are an important part of our oral history.

There are three secrets to Broadfoot's success. First, he is armed with a tape recorder. Second, he conducts thorough background research. And third, he prepares good questions. You can collect valuable information about aboriginal peoples by interviewing someone from a local First Nation.

There are almost thirty distinct aboriginal cultural and language groups in British Columbia. Talking to these people can provide a wonderful opportunity to do further research and deepen your understanding of First Nations. Aboriginal people have traditionally used oral communication as a way of passing on their culture. Stories explaining values and customs of the group are passed down by word of mouth from one generation to the next. All First Nation communities have a rich tradition of stories and legends. You, too, can use the oral interview to discover these beliefs, feelings, and ideas.

Use the sample questionnaire below or create one of your own. Share with the class what you discover in your interviews.

Steps for an Effective Interview

■ Step 1: Purpose

Know your purpose. What information are you

after? In this case, you want to know more about the culture of a local First Nation.

■ Step 2: Research
Prepare well in advance by researching the topic. You need to be well informed to ask intelligent questions.

■ Step 3: Write Questions
Write out questions beforehand. The right question is the only way to get the right information. You can decide on key topics you want to cover, such as adapting to the environment, traditional skills, and contemporary practices. These topics will help you focus your questions.

■ Step 4: Follow-up Questions
Be flexible. Think of secondary or follow-up questions to get deeper explanations. Listen actively to what the person is saying, and encourage him or her to expand on a topic that may uncover some interesting information.

■ Step 5: Arrange the Interview
Make arrangements with the person to be interviewed for a convenient meeting place. Make sure the arrangements are comfortable.

■ Step 6: Record the Interview
Write down as much information as you can, or take an audio or videotape recorder. Always get permission from the person you are interviewing to tape the interview, and know how to operate the machine. Practise before the interview.

■ Step 7: Close the Interview
Finish the interview with an open question, such as "Do you have anything else to add?" Valuable information may be overlooked if you use only your directed questions.

■ Step 8: Expand Your Notes
Expand your notes as soon as possible after the interview.

■ Step 9: Follow-up
Practise good manners. Be on time. Thank the person at the end of the interview, and send a thank-you letter afterwards.

■ Step 10: Share
Share the results of your interview with your classmates.

Sample Questionnaire

1. Could you tell me a story of your people about how the world was created, or why the environment is the way it is? Or is there a story about why the animals are the way they are, or about a great hero or leader of your people?

2. Describe the location and landscape of the traditional lands where your ancestors lived. What were the resources available to people living in the area?

3. Describe how your ancestors adapted to this environment. How did they traditionally manage the resources of the land? How do aboriginal peoples manage environmental resources today?

4. What did the Europeans learn from the First Nations people?

5. In what ways did contact with Europeans change life for your people? Were these changes positive or negative? Why?

6. How were traditional skills, such as building totem poles, passed on from one generation to another?

7. Does your family have any traditional medical treatments that have been passed from generation to generation using plants or animals?

8. How were events such as birth, puberty, marriage, and death traditionally marked in your society? What are the contemporary practices for these events today?

9. Why are land claims so important to aboriginal peoples?

10. What contributions have aboriginal peoples made to British Columbia and to Canada?

11. Do you have any other memories of the way of life of your ancestors that you would like to share?

Western Trade and Exploration

The European exploration and eventual settlement of western Canada really began with the fur trade. Both French and English merchants realized the potential riches in furs. It was the English who first organized the fur trade in western Canada. In 1670, the Hudson's Bay Company received a royal charter for territory called Rupert's Land. This charter gave the company great powers. They were granted the exclusive right to trade in the vast area that drained into Hudson Bay. This was a huge geographic advantage because it provided a direct water route by way of Hudson Bay into the heart of the continent.

In the next few years, the company built trading posts around the shores of Hudson Bay. The most important of these was York Factory, established in 1682 at the mouth of the Nelson River where it drained into Hudson Bay. Each summer ships sailed here from England, bringing goods and supplies to trade with aboriginal peoples. The ships returned to Europe laden down with rich cargoes of furs.

The Hudson's Bay Company soon faced competition, however. Daring traders from New France gradually expanded overland west to the Great Lakes and north towards Hudson Bay. The French tried to offset the geographic advantage that the Hudson's Bay Company enjoyed. Their tactic was to divert furs from the company by building inland posts closer to the aboriginal suppliers. In this way they pushed the fur trade westward in an effort to reach new groups of aboriginal peoples and new fur areas. An adventurous trader, Sieur de La Verendrye, explored routes and established posts at strategic points on Rainy Lake, Lake of the Woods, and Lake Winnipeg, and on the Assiniboine and Red rivers.

After the fall of New France, the competition with the Hudson's Bay Company did not end. The French trading posts and the services of the voyageurs passed into the hands of ambitious Scottish traders based in Montreal. They eventually formed into the giant North West Company in 1787 and brought a new ruthlessness to the fur trade rivalry.

Hudson's Bay Co.'s Cumberland Mission, in the colony of Rupert's Land

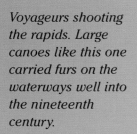

Voyageurs shooting the rapids. Large canoes like this one carried furs on the waterways well into the nineteenth century.

The Fur Trade Rivalry

By 1811, two great trading companies competed fiercely for the limited supplies and markets of the fur trade. On one side was the Hudson's Bay Company based at York Factory, but now with a string of inland forts stretching into the west and northwest. On the other side was the North West Company, based in Montreal and dependent on the rivers and lakes of the prairies to reach their far-flung outposts. The Nor'Westers did not seem to be bothered by the fact that their routes crossed Rupert's Land, the exclusive property of the Hudson's Bay Company.

As the Nor'Westers pushed further west, it became increasingly necessary to build inland posts in which trade goods and furs could be stored. To overcome the problem of distance, the North West Company split its supply line into two parts. Fort William, at the western end of Lake Superior, became the key fort. The "wintering partners" collected furs in the west and brought them to Fort William. Every spring they converged on Fort William out of the wilderness in their small canoes laden with furs. The

"Montreal partners" arrived in Fort William across the Great Lakes in their large freight canoes laden with goods and supplies. Furs and trade goods were exchanged. The wintering partners returned with a new supply of trade goods to exchange with aboriginal peoples for furs. The Montreal partners headed east again with rich cargoes of furs for export. Thus the North West Company adapted its trading methods to overcome the problems of an extended supply line.

The Nor'Westers also discovered a new source of food for its fur brigades. Fur traders required nutritious food to provide energy for the strenuous canoe journeys and the tiring portages. The food had to be easy to carry and keep for long periods of time without spoiling. From the aboriginal peoples the Nor'Westers found the ideal food—pemmican. Pemmican was made of buffalo meat mixed with melted fat and berries. Not only was it nutritious, it was satisfying as well. It became the food that fuelled the fur brigades. Aboriginal peoples of the plains played an essential role by supplying the Nor'Westers with pemmican. They prepared the food supply and deposited it at points where the Nor'Wester voyageurs and boatmen would find it as they journeyed along the waterways. Aboriginal peoples who lived around the posts relied on the pemmican trade as a means of securing manufactured goods. Pemmican became the staple food and a vital part of the Nor'Westers' fur trade.

The fur trade was the greatest single motivating force in the exploration of the west. It was usually the Nor'Westers who discovered new fur areas and new groups of aboriginal peoples with whom to trade. In its rivalry with the Hudson's Bay Company, the Nor'Westers pushed further west to cut off furs destined for the Bay. Eventually, to meet the competition, the Hudson's Bay Company began to build its own inland posts. In response, the North West Company moved further west, only to be followed by the Hudson's Bay Company! Sometimes rival posts were located within sight of each other. At times, violence broke out between the two sides.

The intense rivalry between these two great fur trading companies intensified as the fur supply dwindled. With two prospective buyers, aboriginal peoples could demand more for their furs. The cost of building and maintaining more and more trading posts was also a heavy expense. Profits for both companies declined steadily. However, it was expanding settlements that ultimately led to the decline of the fur trade.

The Selkirk Settlement

In 1811, a wealthy Scottish aristocrat, the Earl of Selkirk, decided to make the Red River into a colony for poor immigrants from the Scottish highlands. Selkirk first bought control of the Hudson's Bay Company. Then he persuaded the company to grant him a vast territory of 300 000 km^2 called Assiniboia. This fertile land was centred along the Red and Assiniboine rivers in what is now parts of Manitoba, Minnesota, and North Dakota. Selkirk's plan was to fill this territory with settlers who would grow crops and raise livestock.

The first group of settlers arrived at York Factory in the fall of 1811. After a bitterly cold winter spent in huts and tents at York Factory, they set out on the exhausting 1100 km journey southward. By the time they reached the site of their future homes, it was too late in the year to plant crops. The colonists survived the

LIFE AS A NOR'WESTER

The fur trade depended on the voyageurs, many of whom were French-Canadian. They came from the settlements along the lower St. Lawrence. They had learned to manage a canoe in all kinds of weather and all kinds of water. They knew their way through the river systems of the continent. They never seemed so happy as when they had a paddle in their hands, and they often sang favourite voyageur songs to keep time as they paddled. They got along well with aboriginal peoples, and some married aboriginal women. They braved snow and sleet, rapids and floods to obtain the furs. Because they had a share in the business, they worked hard so they would earn more profit from the North West Company.

LIFE AT A HUDSON'S BAY COMPANY POST

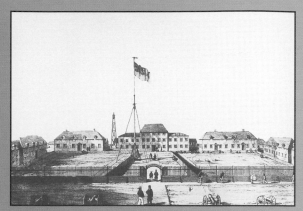

York Factory

York Factory was the central depot for the Hudson's Bay Company. It contained a huge three-storey warehouse in which the company kept a two-year supply of ammunition, food, and trade goods in case the annual supply shipment from England failed to arrive. There were rooms in the warehouse that served as the dining hall and sleeping quarters. The fort also contained smaller buildings, such as a trading shop, workshops, fur storage rooms, and a stone ammunition building. The fort was surrounded by a high wooden stockade.

The head of a post like York Factory was called the Chief Factor. A Chief Trader was responsible for negotiating the buying of the precious fur pelts. In a large fort like York Factory, there was a company doctor who attended to both company employees and local aboriginal peoples. A postmaster distributed the mail that was brought from all the fur trading posts and the annual packets that arrived from England. Clerks and apprentices made up the remainder of the staff who were known as the "company gentlemen."

At the opposite end of the company scale were the labourers whose main job was to transport furs and goods. Sometimes a labourer who knew a number of aboriginal languages was promoted to the position of interpreter. The Company also employed skilled workers such as blacksmiths, boatbuilders, and tailors. Aboriginal peoples living near the fort assisted the company by hunting, cutting wood, loading and unloading goods, and doing odd jobs.

Women had always played an important role in the fur trade. From the earliest days, many fur traders had married aboriginal women. These wives helped the traders learn how to survive in the wilderness and assisted with trade and friendship with aboriginal groups.

The York boat developed by the HBC could hold 80 to 90 fur bales, twice the capacity of a canoe, and was equipped with a sail.

second winter because some aboriginal peoples guided them southward to the buffalo hunting at Pembina. At Pembina there was a small Hudson's Bay post as well as a North West Company building. The newcomers from Scotland had no skill with snowshoes or hunting rifles. They depended on aboriginal peoples to keep them from starvation. In the spring of 1813, their little colony was begun.

Fort Douglas was built near the forks of the Red and Assiniboine rivers where the city of Winnipeg now stands. Fort Daer was built further south near the junction of the Red and Pembina rivers in present-day North Dakota. The early settlers struggled to break the soil because they lacked proper tools. Floods and grasshoppers ruined their crops and food was so scarce that the colonists feared famine.

The Nor'Westers were opposed to the settlement of Assiniboia. They believed that it was a plot by the Hudson's Bay Company to destroy the St. Lawrence-based fur trade. The planned Selkirk Settlement lay right across the North West supply lines between Fort William and the far west. Settlement would drive away the buffalo herds that provided the pemmican and a livelihood for the Métis. Without a secure supply of pemmican, the Nor'Westers would be starved out of business. The North West Company was determined not to let any settlement upset its trade.

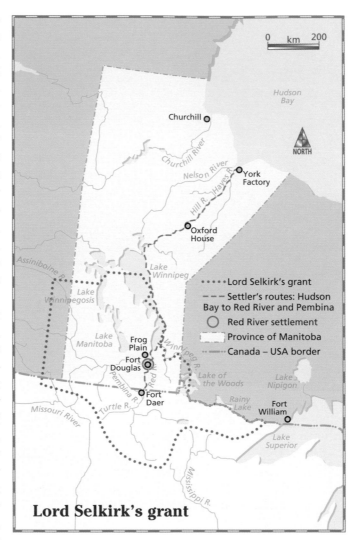

Lord Selkirk's grant

The Nor'Westers and the Métis saw the settlers as intruders who threatened their business and way of life. They were especially angry when Miles Macdonell, the governor of Assiniboia, decided to protect the food supply of the little colony. He issued an order prohibiting the export of any food, including pemmican, from Assiniboia. His order, called the Pemmican Proclamation, enraged the Métis and the fur traders. They depended on the pemmican trade and would have been unable to carry on the fur trade without it. It was time to strike back.

The Métis and Nor'Westers harassed the settlement, burning crops and destroying the buildings of Fort Douglas.

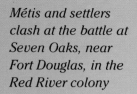

Métis and settlers clash at the battle at Seven Oaks, near Fort Douglas, in the Red River colony

About half of the settlers fled to Upper Canada. But Lord Selkirk had a plan. He sent out a new governor, Robert Semple, to regain control of the settlement. Semple burned the North West Company's post at Fort Gibraltar. He used the remnants of the fort to rebuild Fort Douglas.

The Nor'Westers were furious. In 1816, a group of Métis, led by a North West Company employee, Cuthbert Grant, set out to drive out the colonists once and for all. As they approached Fort Douglas, Governor Semple and twenty-seven settlers rode out to meet them. A skirmish took place on Frog Plain near a grove of trees known as Seven Oaks. Within minutes, Semple and twenty of his followers lay dead.

Meanwhile, Lord Selkirk had been proceeding westward from Upper Canada to aid his struggling colony. This time Selkirk brought in a group of about 100 trained Swiss soldiers to defend his settlers. After that, an uneasy peace reigned in the Red River colony. Roads, bridges, and mills were built and gradually more

settlers arrived. The rivalry that had been destroying the two fur-trading companies was finally ending. The colony was assured of peace when, in 1821, the Hudson's Bay Company bought out the North West Company and the fur trade war officially ended. After 200 years, Montreal's fur trade died. Now all the furs were exported through Hudson Bay.

The colony was further strengthened in 1834 when Lord Selkirk's estate gave control of Assiniboia back to the Hudson's Bay Company. The company used the settlement as its base. The settlers supplied food for all the fur posts to the far west and north. Assiniboia was governed by a governor and a council appointed by the Hudson's Bay Company. By the late 1860s, the population had grown to almost 12 000 people, 87 per cent of whom were Métis. Selkirk had firmly planted a permanent colony in the Canadian West. It was this settlement, not the fur trade, that eventually gave British North America a strong claim to the ownership of the Canadian West.

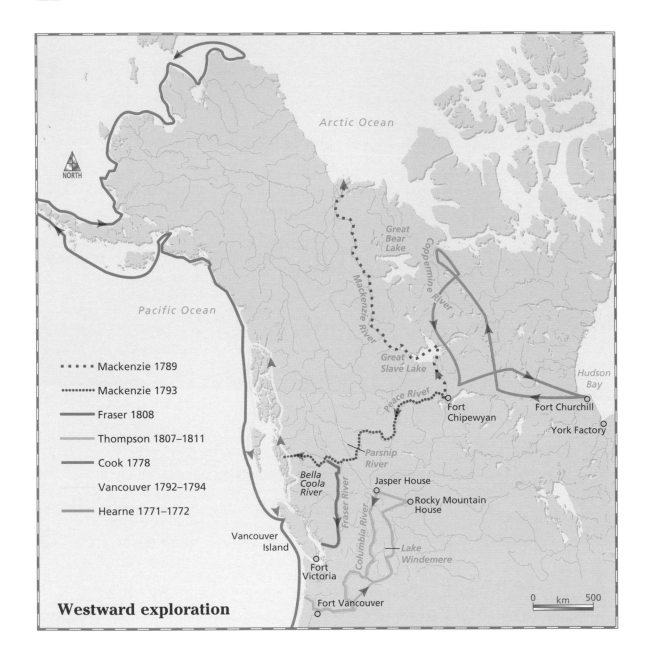

Mackenzie 1789
Mackenzie 1793
Fraser 1808
Thompson 1807–1811
Cook 1778
Vancouver 1792–1794
Hearne 1771–1772

Westward exploration

The Founding of British Columbia

Exploration by Sea

Ships from many countries sailed along the coast of the Pacific Northwest looking for a sea passage through the interior of the continent to the Atlantic. The Russians sailed east from Siberia exploring the coast of Alaska and established a Russian colony there. Meanwhile, the Spanish explored north from Mexico. In 1774, the Spanish ship, the *Santiago*, anchored off Vancouver Island, and two Spanish ships returned there in 1775. In both cases, the Spanish traded with aboriginal peoples for sea otter furs, but they did not land.

Captain James Cook

The first European explorer to land in

Captain James Cook

repairing their ships and observing the Nuu-chah-nulth. Cook was impressed with the trading skills of the Nuu-chah-nulth and traded with them for sea otter cloaks and artifacts such as masks and rattles. After sailing further north without finding the passage, Cook's expedition returned to the Sandwich Islands, now called Hawaii. Cook died there in 1779, but his crew continued on to China. There they found that the sea otter cloaks, which they had been using as blankets, could be sold to the Chinese for large sums of money.

When the journals of Cook's last voyage were published, the high prices paid by the Chinese for sea otter pelts aroused great interest. Soon Nootka Sound appeared on world maps, and merchant ships from London, Boston, and China set out to trade on the Pacific northwest coast. It was the beginning of a rich fur trade that would last for the next half century and it established Britain's presence on the Pacific coast.

what is now British Columbia was the British captain James Cook. He laid claim to this territory for Britain. Cook was exploring the coast hoping to find the western entrance to the Northwest Passage. In 1778, he reached Nootka Sound and established excellent relations with the Nuu-chah-nulth (Nootka) chief, Maquinna. Cook and his crew stayed for almost four weeks,

Captain George Vancouver

The trade in sea otter pelts led to the arrival of many traders, explorers, and

Captain George Vancouver with aboriginal guides going ashore while exploring the west coast

On a flat rock on the edge of Dean Channel, Mackenzie wrote a message in red dye mixed with fish grease: "Alexander Mackenzie, from Canada, by land, the twenty-second of July, one thousand seven hundred and ninety-three." Rain eventually washed away Mackenzie's inscription, but in 1926 the Historic Sites and Monuments Board had it carved in the rock and filled with red cement.

mapmakers on the Pacific coast. It also led to a serious dispute between Spain and Britain over who would control the area. When British ships were seized by the Spanish, Britain threatened war. In 1792, the British government sent Captain George Vancouver to the Pacific coast. Vancouver met and became friends with Spain's Captain Juan Francisco de la Bodega y Quadra. Together they managed to settle the dispute and avert a war. By 1795, the Spanish withdrew from the area, leaving Britain unchallenged on the Pacific coast between California and Alaska.

Together Vancouver and Quadra explored the coast of Vancouver Island, mapping much of the shoreline and naming many places. These voyages established that Vancouver Island was not part of the mainland. Vancouver also wanted to establish whether or not a Northwest Passage actually existed. Each summer

for three years his ships charted the coast from Puget Sound to Alaska, but they found no channel that would lead into the continent. However, the maps created from these travels were so thorough and careful that Vancouver is recognized as one of the world's great mapmakers, and his charts are the basis for some maps still used today.

Exploration by Land

Alexander Mackenzie

On 22 July 1793, while Vancouver was charting the Pacific coast, Alexander Mackenzie became the first European to reach the Pacific over land. He travelled by canoe and on foot from Montreal. When he reached the ocean at Dean Channel, the Nuxalk (Bella Coola) people told him that he had just missed seeing a "large canoe" captained by a man they called Macouba. Mackenzie, the fur trader and explorer from the North West Company, had missed meeting Vancouver, the mapmaker, by just a few weeks.

As Mackenzie travelled across the continent, he hoped to find a river that would flow to the Pacific Ocean. In 1789, he set out from Fort Chipewyan along the Slave River with canoes paddled by Canadian voyageurs and with aboriginal guides and hunters. When they reached Great Slave Lake, they discovered a broad river flowing to the west. Believing it would reach the Pacific, Mackenzie's expedition followed it. For forty days they travelled the river until they reached the ocean. But it was not the Pacific Ocean. Instead it was the Arctic. Discouraged and disillusioned, Mackenzie named it Disappointment River. Today we know it as the mighty Mackenzie River.

In 1792, Mackenzie and his party set out again, this time along the westerly flowing Peace River. By the spring of 1793, they had followed the Peace River and the southerly flowing Parsnip River and had proceeded overland to the turbulent Fraser River. As they struggled along the Fraser, they concluded that its rapids and cascades made it unnavigable. Retracing their path to the West-Road River, they followed this waterway as far west as they could. Local aboriginal peoples told Mackenzie of an easier route that would avoid the rapids and canyons. So they set out on foot to the Bella Coola River following the overland trail aboriginal peoples used to bring fish oil from the coast. Then in canoes borrowed from the aboriginal peoples, Mackenzie and his party followed the Bella Coola until they reached the Pacific Ocean. Mackenzie, who after all his adventures was still only thirty years old, was the first European to reach the Pacific north of Mexico by land.

In spite of his accomplishment, however, Mackenzie returned home discouraged. The fur trade was his business, and the North West Company was not interested in a route to the Pacific unless their voyageurs and canoes could follow it easily.

Simon Fraser

The next person to reach the Pacific was Simon Fraser. Like Mackenzie, Fraser was an employee of the North West Company. Following Mackenzie's route on the Peace River, Fraser crossed overland to the headwaters of the river that bears his name. In 1805, he crossed into what the Nor'Westers called New Caledonia and founded Fort McLeod, the oldest surviving inland settlement in British Columbia.

In the spring of 1808, Fraser and his voyageurs set out on one of the most dangerous and hazardous journeys in the history of exploration—down the Fraser River. Walled in on both sides by sheer rock cliffs, the explorers were flung along the swift-flowing river. At every turn, the canoes were in danger of being smashed against the rocks or overturned in the rapids. They were forced to abandon their canoes at the narrow gorge known as Hell's Gate. There they had to carry their baggage over narrow scaffolds,

Simon Fraser and his party on part of their heroic exploration of the Fraser River. Fraser later wrote in his diary, "I have been for a long period among the Rocky Mountains, but have never seen anything to equal this country…. We had to pass where no human being should venture."

bridges, and ladders high above the river. This portage was every bit as dangerous as navigating the waters of the river below. Yet the expedition members survived, and after obtaining some canoes from local aboriginal peoples, they continued on to the coast. On 2 July 1808, they reached the mouth of the Fraser River and first sighted the mountains of Vancouver Island. Like Mackenzie, however, Simon Fraser returned home disappointed. The Fraser River, which was later named for him, had proven to be too turbulent and dangerous for fur traders.

David Thompson taking an observation

David Thompson

While Simon Fraser was looking for a canoe route to the Pacific, David Thompson, another employee of the North West Company, was exploring the Rocky Mountains in search of another possible route. Thompson entered the fur trade as a young apprentice, first working for the Hudson's Bay Company. After learning the skills of a surveyor and mapmaker, Thompson went to work for the rival company, the Nor'Westers.

In 1807, Thompson reached the Columbia River and built a trading fort at Lake Windemere. Using the fort as a base, he explored the region to the south and west, and discovered the Kootenay River system. By 1811, Thompson had reached the mouth of the Columbia River, only to find that American fur traders had already established a fort there. He had, however, demonstrated that there was a feasible transportation route to the mouth of the Columbia River.

Mackenzie, Fraser, and Thompson had laid claim to what is today British Columbia. The North West Company now controlled the fur trade in the region west of the mountains. When they bought

out the American traders at the mouth of the Columbia River in 1813, the whole area from the Peace River to the Columbia was under the company's control. In 1821, the Hudson's Bay Company took over the North West Company, and established Fort Vancouver on the lower Columbia as its western headquarters. The twenty years following the merger were relatively stable ones. Hudson's Bay Company ships sailed up and down the coast and furs were exported across the oceans to Britain or China.

In 1843, the Hudson's Bay Company decided to build a fort on the southern tip of Vancouver Island. James Douglas arrived on the company's steamship *Beaver* and set about building a trading post. He named it Victoria in honour of the young queen of England. But even before Fort Victoria was finished, the fur trade on the west coast had started to change. The number of fur-bearing animals was declining, along with European demand for furs.

Britain was in a dispute with the United States over the ownership of the area west of the Rocky Mountains. The United States insisted that all the land between California and the southern border of Alaska was US territory. They threatened to go to war, proclaiming the slogan "Fifty-four Forty or Fight"—the 54 40' being the southernmost border of

Alaska. The Hudson's Bay Company hoped to hold the border at the Columbia River. However, when the Oregon Treaty between Britain and the United States was completed in 1846, the border was set at the 49th parallel. There was a slight diversion at the western end to include Vancouver Island and the new port at Victoria in British territory.

The Founding of the Colony on Vancouver Island

In 1849, Vancouver Island became a crown colony. It was the first regular outpost of British government in North America west of Upper Canada. James Douglas was appointed governor while retaining his post as chief factor for the Hudson's Bay Company. In 1856, an elected assembly with seven representatives was established.

Douglas was eager to see the colony grow around the outpost of Victoria. By 1852, there were about 500 settlers on Vancouver Island. Between 1850 and 1854, Douglas signed fourteen treaties with Coast Salish bands on the island. In exchange for the surrender of about 927 km^2 of land, the government paid the Coast Salish with blankets and other goods. When money to purchase more land ran out, Douglas did the next best thing—he had reserves surveyed for the aboriginal peoples. These reserves included their villages, fishing areas, and sacred burial grounds. The Douglas treaties tried to deal responsibly and fairly with the First Nations peoples. Later, it was argued that by signing these treaties, Douglas was acknowledging that aboriginal peoples owned the land being taken over for settlement.

The population of Vancouver Island colony increased slowly as a few settlers established farms along the southern shore. The lumber industry began when the first sawmill was built at Victoria in 1848. Soon the mill was exporting sawn lumber to San Francisco. The commercial fishery began with barrels of salt salmon exported to Hawaii. Coal was discovered in the northern part of Vancouver Island at Nanaimo. By 1850, the basic primary industries of British Columbia—logging, fishing, and mining—were established.

By 1858, the population of the colony numbered between 700 and 800 non-aboriginal people, largely centred around Victoria. The town had a few shops and houses, a stockaded fort with warehouses, and a harbour with wharves. Then something happened to change the northwest coast forever—gold!

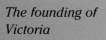

The founding of Victoria

DEVELOPING SKILLS: USING MAPS AS VISUAL ORGANIZERS

Suppose you need directions to a friend's home for a party. You can ask for verbal directions—whether to go north, south, east, or west, where to turn, or what landmarks to look for. But if the route is complicated, it will help to have a sketch map. A map is a way of visually presenting or organizing information.

You've just read about the land and sea explorations of what is today British Columbia. How far did the explorers extend their explorations by 1811? You could give an accurate picture of westward expansion by recording and summarizing information on a map. Every map must have the following four important elements to be complete. Without these, it would be difficult for anyone to use the map.

■ 1: Title

The title of a map should describe the area the map covers and accurately summarize the information it presents. If you were describing the fur trade in the west, why would "The Fur Trade" be a poor title? Why would "Westward Expansion of the Fur Trade between 1778 and 1811" be a better title?

■ 2: Direction

Direction is indicated by a compass. Most maps are drawn with north at the top. If north is at the top of the map, then you know south is in the opposite direction, east is to the right, and west is to the left. Try this quiz. On the map on page 82, what direction is Hudson Bay from Great Slave Lake? What direction is Jasper House from Rocky Mountain House?

■ 3: Scale

The scale tells distance and size represented on the map compared with distance and size represented on the earth's surface. When you use the scale on a map, you can measure the approximate distance between two places or the rough size of a country. Look at the map on page 82. Each division on the scale represents 500 km.

Use the scale to determine the approximate distance from Fort Churchill to Fort Chipewyan.

■ 4: Key or Legend

Information can be placed on maps using symbols that are identified in a legend. A symbol represents an idea, person, group, or thing. Colours are also used to represent information. On a political map, for example, colour can be used to indicate different provinces, states, regions, or countries.

Mapping the Westward Expansion of the Fur Trade

1. Start with an outline map of western Canada and the northwestern United States. Give your map a title, and be sure that it includes direction and a scale.

2. Locate Fort Chipewyan and the Mackenzie River. Label the fort and the river. Choose an appropriate colour to indicate Mackenzie's exploration to the Arctic and indicate the year this expedition took place. Be sure to identify the colours in your legend.

3. Label the rivers and mark the route Mackenzie explored in 1793 using a different colour. Mark the spot where Mackenzie reached the Pacific and left his inscription. Add this information to the legend.

4. Using a different colour, trace Simon Fraser's route to the Pacific. Remember to indicate the year. Add Fraser's journey to the legend.

5. Trace David Thompson's route on the map using a fourth colour. Label the river and update the legend.

6. Review the explorations of Hudson's Bay Company employee Samuel Hearne in 1771-72 on the map on page 82. Mark his route in a fifth colour. Label it and update the legend.

7. Add the following forts to the map: Fort Churchill, York Factory, Fort Vancouver, Fort Victoria.

8. Identify the First Nations peoples of British Columbia that these explorers may have encountered. Add their names and their territories to your map.

9. Review your map. People should have a clear picture of the westward expansion of the fur trade from your map. Exchange your map with a classmate and have your partner check that your map is clear, accurate, and complete.

THE GOLD RUSH

May 18, 1862 Williams Creek

Dear Joe
I am well and so are all the rest of the boys. I am writing you a few lines to let you know that I am well, and doing well-making two to three thousand dollars a day! Times good! Grub high. Whisky bad. Money plenty!

Yours truly
William Cunningham

Imagine it is 1862. You are living at home in England. A few years earlier, your older brother William set off to seek his fortune in North America. You haven't heard from him for months. Then one day, out of the blue, you receive a postcard. Your brother has become a gold miner in British Columbia! It sounds like there are great fortunes to be made mining gold. You decide to join your brother in British Columbia as soon as you can. The idea of adventure and getting rich appeals to you. But how will you get there and how long will it take? A visit to one of the shipping companies will give you the answers you need.

There are three main routes to British Columbia. The fastest, but most expensive, route is to sail from England to Panama. There you must cross the isthmus of Panama. You get off the ship at Colon on the Atlantic side and cross the isthmus by stagecoach. On the Pacific side, you board another ship at Darien. From Darien, you sail north to San Francisco, where you transfer to another ship to take you north to Victoria. From there, you travel by steamship to the mainland of British Columbia. The entire journey could take six to eight weeks.

A cheaper, but much slower, way to get to the gold mines is to sail all the way

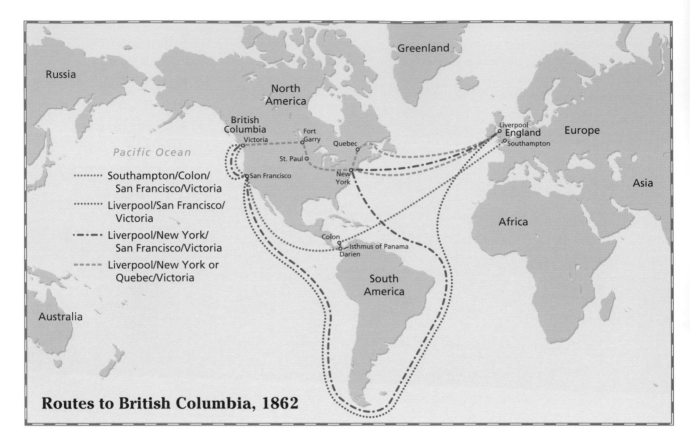

Routes to British Columbia, 1862

Russia

Greenland

North America

British Columbia
Victoria

Fort Garry

Quebec

St. Paul

Liverpool
England
Southampton

Europe

Pacific Ocean

San Francisco

New York

Asia

········· Southampton/Colon/
San Francisco/Victoria

········· Liverpool/San Francisco/
Victoria

·–·–· Liverpool/New York/
San Francisco/Victoria

– – – Liverpool/New York or
Quebec/Victoria

Colon
Darien
Isthmus of Panama

Africa

Australia

South
America

around the southern tip of South America and up the coast to San Francisco and Victoria. But this trip could take four or five months!

A third route takes you by steamer to Quebec or New York and then over land to British Columbia. This could be a very long and difficult trip. You travel from Quebec or New York by train on American railways to St. Paul, Minnesota. Then you head north by stage and steamboat to Fort Garry. There you join a small party of Overlanders. These hardy travellers set off westward across the prairies in carts and wagons, taking horses and oxen with them. There are no roads, only trails to follow. There are rivers to cross and many other perils and extraordinary hardships along the way. The wagon train is often a kilometre long as it straggles over the prairies. Every night the Overlanders imitate the custom of the Métis and form their carts into a triangle

for security. Finally you face the Rocky Mountains. The only way over the mountains is to find a pass, such as the Athabasca Pass, and make the climb on

Catherine Schubert was the only woman among a group of goldseekers, known as the Overlanders of '62. She gave birth to a daughter the day she arrived in Kamloops.

foot or snowshoe. The last part of the trip is by raft down the Columbia River, with its dangerous rapids, to Fort Vancouver. In any weather, this is the longest, most exhausting, and most dangerous route to get to British Columbia!

In the 1850s and 1860s, the people in Canada were preoccupied with the union of the colonies. But the people on the Pacific coast were busy with something else—gold!

In 1857, aboriginal peoples on the Thompson River in British Columbia presented gold nuggets in exchange for goods in the Hudson's Bay store in Kamloops. The Hudson's Bay Company official did not know the value of the mineral. He sent the gold nuggets to James Douglas, his boss in Victoria. Douglas quickly sent word back to get as much of this metal as he could: it was gold!

The Gold Rush Is On!

In no time, the word spread: "There is gold on the Fraser River!" Miners who had been digging in the gold mines of California packed up and headed north.

Business people sold out and joined the crowd going to British Columbia to get rich. The gold rush in the valley of the Fraser River had begun.

Since 1849, Vancouver Island had been a British crown colony. The Hudson's Bay Company was responsible for settling the island. But the company was more interested in the fur trade than encouraging settlement. In 1858, when the gold rush started, the settlement of Fort Victoria on Vancouver Island was a remote little colony of only a few hundred people devoted to the fur trade.

Suddenly that summer, more than 20 000 miners swarmed into town. On one day alone 2800 people arrived! Strangers piled into the trading post to buy food and equipment. The quiet little town of Victoria was transformed into a bustling city of tents, shacks, and stores. The price of lots in Victoria skyrocketed from $50 to $1500.

Miners left from Victoria for the Fraser River on anything that would float. Fistfights broke out for places on the steamers. Those who were too impatient to wait for the steamships set out in canoes, rowboats, and even on rafts.

The overland route to the Cariboo goldfields

Panning for gold in the Cariboo goldfields, British Columbia, 1862

At sandbars along the Fraser River, miners began **panning** for gold. This was the easiest and simplest method. The miners used a metal pan with sloping sides. They loosened the gravel in the streambed with their pickaxes and shovelled it into their pans. Then they filled the pan with water and tilted it away from themselves slightly. Since gold is so heavy, it sinks to the bottom of the pan. The miners kept tilting the pan until all the light gravel had washed out. All that was left was fine black sand and, if the miner was lucky, flakes of gold.

A faster method of mining gold was **rocking**. Miners would build a box that was wide at the top and sloped in at the bottom. It was built on rockers much like a cradle. While one miner shovelled sand and gravel into the box, the other poured in water to wash it through. At the top was a screen where big nuggets of gold were caught. Below that, a piece of blanket cloth caught the gold flakes that sifted through from above. One rocker might produce gold dust worth $100 in a day. By the end of the summer of 1858, $500 000 worth of gold had been taken out of the Fraser River area.

James Douglas was governor of Vancouver Island. Although he had no power on the Fraser River, he believed that as Queen Victoria's representative he had to do all he could to keep law and order there. The mainland, still called New Caledonia, was without a government, though it was recognized as British territory. During the summer of 1858, Douglas made several trips up the Fraser when he heard there was stealing and quarrelling over claims. He was accompanied by a group of Royal Engineers armed with a cannon. He warned rowdy miners that they were in British territory and must obey British law or be punished.

The British Parliament, hearing of the gold rush, passed an act creating the colony of British Columbia on the mainland, a name chosen by Queen Victoria herself. James Douglas was appointed governor of British Columbia as well as of Vancouver Island. He was, however, expected to give up his connection with the Hudson's Bay Company. At the same time, the British appointed Matthew Baillie Begbie as the colony's judge. Together, Douglas and Begbie kept law

CHARACTERS IN CANADIAN HISTORY: JUDGE MATTHEW BAILLIE BEGBIE

Judge Begbie

Matthew Baillie Begbie was British Columbia's first judge. He was sent out from England in November 1858. He was the only judge in an area expanding hundreds of thousands of square kilometres. His main task was to protect aboriginal peoples who resented the intrusion of the miners, and to keep law and order among the miners.

Begbie would hold court in a saloon, a cabin, or even on horseback in the middle of the wilderness! He was a tough judge. After a fair trial, he would give the order to immediately string up a murderer on the nearest tree. The legend of Judge Begbie soon spread around the campfires and saloons. He was known as the "hanging judge."

Although Judge Begbie's punishments often seemed swift and harsh, he was dealing with an unruly group of miners. Most were armed with pistols, knives, and other weapons. It was fear of being brought before Judge Begbie that kept many possible lawbreakers out of trouble.

When British Columbia joined Confederation, Judge Begbie became the chief justice for the new province. In 1874, he was knighted by Queen Victoria for his contribution to ensuring that British Columbia's gold rush was an orderly one.

and order in the gold rush in British Columbia.

A New Find: The Cariboo

A few years after the start of the gold rush, a great new gold find was made farther up the Fraser River in the Cariboo Mountains. Once again, American miners began pouring into British Columbia. In 1862, a British sailor named Billy Barker arrived. With his friends he started digging down into the earth in the hope of finding gold. At 16 m they discovered some gold deposits. They kept on digging. Another 8 m down Barker found a rich vein of gold. In the first forty-eight hours,

he took out $1000 worth of gold. The boom was on again!

Within a few weeks, a collection of shanties sprang up around the Barker claim. The settlement, named Barkerville in Billy's honour, grew into a town of 10 000. Money flowed freely in the hotels, music halls, dance halls, saloons, gambling houses, and stores. Prices of the day were skyhigh! A barrel of flour cost $300 and potatoes cost $20 a kg. For ten years, the Cariboo boomed, and British Columbia became world famous as miners rushed in hoping to strike it rich.

Governor Douglas decided that a good wagon road was needed along the Fraser River to Barkerville. The Royal Engineers who built the Cariboo Road had an almost impossible task. In some places they had to blast through solid rock. In others they had to span the river with high bridges on wooden **trestles**. When the rock did not give way, they had to build the road out over the roaring river supported on **cribbings**. The cribbings were huge trees piled high on top of each other to provide a solid base for the road.

When the road was finished, it opened the entire Cariboo for settlement. Miners moved in their families. Ranchers drove herds of cattle north, launching the important cattle industry that still exists today.

But the gold rushes and the building of the Cariboo Road had a negative impact on aboriginal peoples. Gold was usually found in remote areas. But it was in these remote regions that aboriginal peoples could still maintain their traditional way of life. Miners ignored aboriginal land claims in their rush to exploit the land for its gold. The building of

roads damaged the remaining fur-trading areas. Miners interfered with the aboriginal peoples' salmon weirs, raided their villages, and even looted their burial sites. On top of this, smallpox broke out among the Tsilhqot'in (Chilcotin) in 1862. The government provided no protection for aboriginal peoples as miners and settlers invaded their lands and upset their traditional ways of supporting themselves.

The Cariboo Road cost almost $1 million to build. It was more than the new colony could afford. As the gold began to run out, hundreds of people left the region. Both colonies, Vancouver Island and British Columbia, suffered from financial problems. People realized that it would be cheaper if they had one assembly and functioned as one colony. In 1866, the two colonies joined together as British Columbia.

Seventeen Mile Bluff

THE GREAT CAMEL CATASTROPHE

One of the last camels on the Cariboo Road. Can you see why they were not suited to mountain travel?

The Great Camel Catastrophe

Before the Cariboo Road was carved out, a herd of twenty-three camels was imported to haul freight into the Cariboo gold fields. It was said that the camels were capable of packing much heavier loads than mules. They were also supposed to be able to survive in extreme summer heat and bitterly cold winters. It seemed they were just what the gold rush needed.

The experiment seemed doomed from the beginning. No sooner were the animals unloaded than two broke loose and wandered for months in the lush forests. They caused the death of one old miner who met one on a lonely trail and dropped dead from a heart attack.

The miners soon discovered that the camels had difficulty travelling the rocky trails because their feet were used to desert sands. Their drivers did not like the camels because their stench stuck to their clothing. The owners hoped that the camels' long legs would permit them to wade through deep snow. But it wasn't to be. Several camels and drivers were lost in fierce blizzards.

When spring came, there was more trouble. The camels spooked the mule trains and caused some of the mules to plunge to their deaths in the deep canyons. The owners of the mule trains were outraged. Before guns started blazing, the camel project was abandoned and the animals were sent back to Victoria. The last remaining camel from the experiment died on a farm in 1905.

DEVELOPING SKILLS: PREPARING A RESEARCH REPORT

You are about to start on a bicycle trip and you discover something is wrong with your bike. What do you do? Cancel your trip? No. Head to the local library! You can borrow a bicycle repair manual that gives step-by-step instructions on how to fix your bike.

Resource centres are valuable sources of information on just about any topic. The trick is to find the information you need quickly and efficiently. You are asked to write a research report about the gold rush. What do you do? Here are some key steps to follow:

■ Step 1: Purpose

1. Be sure you understand your assignment. For example, you need to know that a **report** summarizes and presents important information on a particular topic. It is different from an **essay**, which develops a particular point of view or argument. Also ask yourself these questions:

   • What exactly am I being asked to do?

   • When is the assignment due?

   • How long should it be?

• How is it to be presented—as a written report, an oral presentation, etc.?
• How will it be evaluated?

Highlight key words in your assignment so you are clear about what you need to do.

Step 2: Preparation

2. Often you will have options. You may be given a choice of topics, for example. Choose your topic carefully. Ask yourself:
   • Will I find this topic interesting?
   • Is this topic manageable?
   • Will I be able to find resources?
   • Will I have enough time to complete the assignment?
   • Is the topic specific or too broad? Do I need to define it more carefully?

Suppose your topic is the gold rush in the Cariboo. By asking these questions, you will come to the conclusion that this topic is too broad and therefore unmanageable. So much has been written about the Cariboo that it would be impossible to cover it all. You need to define your topic more carefully. You might decide to focus on the methods of mining for gold during the Cariboo gold rush.

Step 3: Process

3. Once you have a clear idea of your topic, you can start your research. Use the card or computer catalogue in your resource centre to identify possible resources. The catalogue is the nucleus of any library. It lists all resources by author, title, and subject.

   For information on methods of mining used during the gold rush, there are several possible subjects to look under. You could look under "mining," "Cariboo gold rush," "panning for gold," or "gold." [HINT: Always have a pencil and paper with you when using the catalogue. Jot down the call numbers of the books so you can locate them on the shelves.]

   Check periodical indexes and computer databases for magazines, audio-visual resources, newspaper reports, and journal articles. Check the vertical information files. You will probably be surprised by the amount of information you discover.

4. Next, get an overview of your topic by browsing and skimming through a number of the resources you locate. The idea is to familiarize yourself with the information available on your topic. Then you can decide where you will focus your attention in your research. For example, you may discover that encyclopedia articles, special reference books on the gold rush, and films are the best sources of information.

5. Make point-form notes from your resources. Try to use your own words. Gather references for illustrations as well. Always note the source of the information (author, title, date, and page number).

Step 4: Product

6. Once you have gathered your information, develop a working outline. This becomes the framework of your report. Organize your information into a few main ideas.

   For example, you may decide to focus on three methods of mining for gold. Enter your main ideas on an organizer like the one on page 97. Your subpoints would include descriptions of each of the methods, illustrations, and information on how they were used. As a conclusion, you could present your ideas on how effective the methods were for the miners.

7. Prepare a draft copy of your report. Decide on an introduction that will grab the reader's or listener's attention. It should give a clear and concise statement of the focus topic.

   Develop each of your main ideas or subtopics. Be sure the main idea is clearly expressed in a topic sentence and that the subpoints refer to and develop the main idea. Put the main ideas in the most effective order, leaving the best idea for last.

   Write a conclusion that summarizes your main points, reinforces what you have said, and leaves your audience with something interesting to think about.

8. Edit your draft. Be sure that:
   • you have met the requirements of the assignment
   • the report is organized logically and makes sense to the reader/listener

Names in Group: _____	Teacher's Name: _____	
_____	Class: _____	
_____	Due Date: _____	

Focus Topic/Question: Panning for gold in the Cariboo

Main Idea/Subtopic:	Main Idea/Subtopic:	Main Idea/Subtopic:
Panning for gold	*Rocking for gold*	*Sluice box method*
Subpoints:	Subpoints:	Subpoints:

Conclusion:

- the sentences vary in length and structure
- the spelling, grammar, capitalization, and punctuation are correct.

9. Consider a variety of possible formats as indicated below or a combination of ways to present your research report.

■ Step 5: Personal Learning

10. Once you have completed or presented your report, reflect on it. Evaluate what you have done and think about what you might do differently next time to improve your work. Classmates or your teacher can help you with this evaluation process.

Try It!

Choose one of the following topics on the Cariboo gold rush and prepare a research report:

i)   methods of mining
ii) life in Barkerville
iii) life in a miner's home
iv) sourdough
v)   law and order in the goldfields
vi) the importance of the Cariboo gold rush to British Columbia
vii) characters of the Cariboo gold rush.

Oral	Visual	Written
• panel discussion	• slide show or overhead transparencies	• report
• dramatization		• booklet
• role play	• picture story	• newspaper
• radio broadcast	• models/diagrams	• letter or diary
• interview	• charts, graphs, maps	• poem
• talk with visuals		• play
	• film or video	• memoir
	• bulletin board display	

Two Colonies or One?

James Douglas retired as governor of the two Pacific colonies in 1863. He was succeeded by two governors, one on the island and one on the mainland. However, the gold rush boom had ended and the population was declining. Soon the British government decided that the duplication of services in two colonies was too expensive. In 1866, the colonies were encouraged to merge to become the united colonies of British Columbia. A twenty-three member council was established, but only nine of its members were elected, four from the island and five from the mainland. British Columbia still did not have full representative and responsible government.

At first, the new capital was located in New Westminster, a rather rustic town on the mainland. In 1868, it was moved to Victoria, which was considered by government officials to be a more comfortable place to live. The capital has remained there ever since. One of the chief advocates of the move was Amor de Cosmos.

CHARACTERS IN CANADIAN HISTORY: AMOR DE COSMOS

Amor de Cosmos was a colourful figure. Born William Smith in Nova Scotia, he made his way to Victoria by way of the California goldfields. He changed his name to Amor de Cosmos, meaning "lover of the universe." As owner and editor of his own newspaper, he launched bitter attacks on the ruling political leaders, whom he once called "vain, puffed up, tyrannical, corrupt, short-witted, conceited mummies and numbskulls!" De Cosmos had seen Nova Scotia become the first of the British North American colonies to gain responsible government in 1848. He wanted to see the same system established in British Columbia. In 1863, de Cosmos was elected to the assembly of Vancouver Island. Using his powers of oratory, he and another member once took turns speaking for twenty-six hours until they wore down the majority opposed to their motion. It was largely through de Cosmos's persuasive efforts that Vancouver Island and British Columbia were united.

Amor de Cosmos

De Cosmos was also an influential promoter of union with Canada. Shortly after British Columbia entered Confederation, de Cosmos became the province's premier. He also served in federal politics for eleven years as a Member of Parliament from British Columbia. In Ottawa, however, he never emerged as a national leader as his interests were confined to issues affecting only British Columbia. Still, Amor de Cosmos's greatest legacy is that he helped make a "dominion from sea to sea" a reality.

ACTIVITIES

Check Your Understanding

1. Add these new words to your *Factfile*.

   culture • cultural area • coniferous • potlatch • pemmican • nomadic • royal charter • North West Company • voyageur • Chief Factor • Chief Trader • Northwest Passage • New Caledonia • Hell's Gate • Fort McLeod • Fifty-four Forty or Fight • Oregon Treaty • Overlanders • gold rush • panning for gold • rocking for gold • Cariboo Road

2. Why was the early period of contact between aboriginal peoples and Europeans generally friendly? Why did things eventually change?

3. How was the culture of aboriginal peoples of the Pacific Northwest Coast influenced by their physical environment?

4. Why was pemmican so essential to the fur trade and to aboriginal peoples?

5. What were the living and working conditions for people in the fur trade? Illustrate your answer in a mural using words and sketches.

6. In an organizer, summarize the explorations of British Columbia by Cook, Vancouver, Mackenzie, Fraser, and Thompson under the following headings: Time period of the explorations, Areas explored, and Contributions.

7. Use a comparison organizer to describe the colony of Vancouver Island before and after the discovery of gold in the Cariboo.

8. Why were fur traders and Métis opposed to settlement at the Red River?

Confirm Your Learning

9. Role-play a meeting of pre-European contact aboriginal peoples from two distinct cultural areas of Canada (for example, people from the Pacific Northwest Coast and the Plains). Have each group explain to the other their environment and how their lifestyle has been adapted to this environment.

10. How did the Nor'Westers organize themselves to challenge their rival, the Hudson's Bay Company? How effective were they?

11. Create a mind map to show how the crossroads location of the Red River settlement created problems between fur companies, aboriginal peoples, and settlers.

12. Read the following eyewitness account of the incident at Seven Oaks:

    In the course of the winter (1816) we were much alarmed by reports that the Métis were assembling in all parts of the North for the purpose of driving us away.

> *On the afternoon of 19 June, a man in the watch-house called out that the Métis were coming. The governor said, "We must go out and meet these people; let 20 men follow me." (28 actually went)*
>
> *We had not proceeded far before the Métis, on horseback, came forward and surrounded us. We retreated a few steps backwards and then saw a man named Boucher ride up to us calling out. "What do you want?" the governor asked. Boucher answered, "We want our fort."*
>
> *They were by this time near each other, and spoke too low for me to hear. I saw the governor take hold of Boucher's gun, and almost immediately a general discharge of firearms took place; but whether it began on our side or that of the enemy, it was impossible to distinguish. In a few minutes almost all our people were either killed or wounded.*

Statement respecting the Earl of Selkirk's settlement on the Red River. London 1817.

Use a decision-making model to help you decide what other options Semple could have followed that might have avoided bloodshed. In groups, follow the steps in the decision-making process. Come to a group decision on this issue and role-play it before the class.

13. Why would violence and lawlessness develop in the goldfields? What did Governor Douglas and Judge Begbie do to control the violence? How successful were they?

14. Outline the contributions made by Amor de Cosmos to the development of the province of British Columbia.

Challenge Your Mind

15. Set up penpals with a First Nations school or band.

16. "The fur trade proved to be the greatest single motivating force in westward exploration." Discuss.

17. In groups of two or three, draw political cartoons that describe the rivalry between the Hudson's Bay Company and the North West Company.

18. Debate: James Douglas deserves the title of "founder of British Columbia."

19. Create a visual display of various aspects of the gold rush in British Columbia.

20. People have always been excited by the prospect of finding gold. Columbus sailed across the ocean looking for gold. Kings and queens promised rewards to anyone who could change less valuable metals into gold.

    Below are some thoughts that people have had about gold through the centuries. Explain what each of these quotations means. With which ones do you agree? With which ones do you disagree? Why? Find other sayings about gold, or make up a short saying of your own.
    • All that glitters is not gold. (*Proverb*)
    • Gold is good and learning is much better. (*Proverb*)

- It is observed of gold that to have it is to be in fear, and to want it is to be in danger. (*S. Johnson*)
- Gold begets in brethren hate,
  Gold in families debate,
  Gold does friendship separate,
  Gold does civil wars create. (*A. Cowley*)
- I despise gold; it hath persuaded many a man to evil. (*Plautus*)

CHAPTER 4

Manitoba and British Columbia Enter Confederation

THE GREATEST LAND DEAL IN HISTORY

Confederation in 1867 established the new nation of Canada. In the years following, thoughts turned to expanding the nation westward into the vast lands controlled by the Hudson's Bay Company. People dreamed of turning that land into farms where their children could settle.

The Hudson's Bay Company had owned the vast territory known as **Rupert's Land** since 1670. The territory included all the land drained by the rivers that flowed into Hudson Bay. For almost 200 years no one, except aboriginal peoples and fur traders, cared much about Rupert's Land. Then, about the time of Confederation, Canadians began to think seriously about settling the West.

The Hudson's Bay Company lands also included the **Red River Settlement** around Fort Garry (near the present city of Winnipeg). About 12 000 settlers

York boats arrive at Norway House

lived in the colony. The settlers had sent petitions to London protesting the way the Hudson's Bay Company was ruling their settlement. They felt they did not have the rights and privileges British subjects should enjoy. They preferred to be part of Canada.

Canada's new prime minister, John A. Macdonald, feared that Canada and Britain would lose the West if they did not act. In a letter in 1865 he wrote:

In January 1870, John A. Macdonald sent Donald Smith to report on the unrest at Red River. A crowd gathered to hear him explain his commission at Fort Garry.

"I am perfectly willing to leave Rupert's Land a wilderness for the next half century, but I fear that if the Canadians do not go in, the Yankees will."

Canada decided to send delegates to England to find out if the Hudson's Bay Company would sell its empire to Canada. The company was in no hurry to give up its claim to the land. But finally a price was agreed upon. The Hudson's Bay Company would be paid $300 000 and keep 5 per cent of the fertile land, or about 2.5 million hectares. Eventually, it would sell parts of that land to settlers. The company also kept its trading posts and the land immediately around them. The British government also agreed to transfer the North-Western Territory to Canada.

The whole region was to be transferred to Canada on 1 December 1869 and renamed the **North-West Territories**. Canada decided the North-West Territories would be ruled by a Lieutenant-Governor and council appointed by the federal government. Thus one of the greatest land deals in history was completed. Before its third birthday, Canada would stretch almost from sea to sea.

Trouble at Red River

The expansion westward was not as simple as the deal suggested, however. Long before the Hudson's Bay lands were sold to Canada in 1869, aboriginal peoples had lived in and travelled over this vast territory. Most aboriginal peoples in the West were nomadic, moving from place to place hunting buffalo and trapping fur-bearing animals.

The few European settlers in the region were Hudson's Bay Company employees working at scattered trading posts. Their job was to buy furs from the aboriginal peoples in exchange for goods. Only at Red River was there a large populated settlement in the 1860s.

Many of these settlers were farmers or merchants.

The **Métis** formed the largest group living in the Red River Settlement. The Métis nation, as they called themselves, originated in western Canada during the fur trade era. The Métis were people of mixed aboriginal and European heritage. They had a distinct culture that was a blend of European and aboriginal ways.

The buffalo hunt was central to the Métis way of life. For part of the year they left their small farms along the Red and Assiniboine rivers to follow the herds of buffalo. The hunt provided the Métis with their main source of income. The hides and meat were sold to the Hudson's Bay Company. They also supplied fur traders with pemmican, the dried buffalo meat used by traders on long winter trips.

In the early days, the Métis formed the backbone of the fur trade in the West. Because they spoke English or French and some aboriginal languages, they acted as agents between other aboriginal groups and Europeans. They bought furs from aboriginal peoples and sold them to the Hudson's Bay Company agents. Some transported goods in their Red River carts in the days before the railway reached the West. Often they worked as interpreters and guides for the Hudson's Bay Company. Many journeys into western Canada would have been impossible without the skills of Métis guides.

Background to Rebellion

The Hudson's Bay Company had withdrawn its rule from Rupert's Land in January 1869. The Canadian government was not entitled to establish rule until December. For almost twelve months, the people of the territory had no legal government. Who would protect their rights?

On sunny June days in 1869, crews of Canadian surveyors appeared on the farms of the Métis in the Red River Settlement. The Canadian government was eager to survey the land recently bought from the Hudson's Bay Company. This was ground the Métis people thought was theirs to use.

The Métis were told by the surveyors that the land would be marked out in large squares. This was how the land was

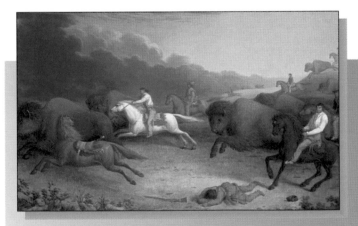

Métis running the buffalo

A Red River cart on the prairie. The Red River carts were made entirely of wood, with the parts held together by wooden pegs and strips of rawhide.

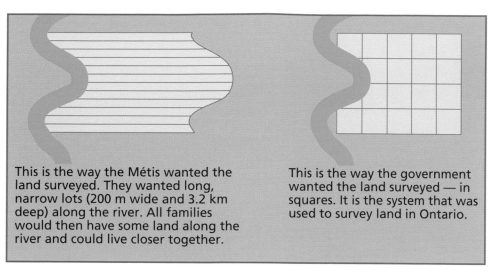

This is the way the Métis wanted the land surveyed. They wanted long, narrow lots (200 m wide and 3.2 km deep) along the river. All families would then have some land along the river and could live closer together.

This is the way the government wanted the land surveyed — in squares. It is the system that was used to survey land in Ontario.

The land survey controversy in the Red River Settlement

divided in Ontario. Métis farms were laid out in narrow strips facing the rivers, in the same way the people of New France had laid out farms along the St. Lawrence River. This would mean an end to their narrow river farms.

Most of the Métis had not bought the land they lived on. Instead their families had settled the land and established small farms. This was a form of ownership that was recognized by the Métis nation, yet it did not meet European ideas of ownership. For the Métis, the

Louis Riel

thought of settlers coming in and taking over their lands was alarming. Many were also disturbed by the rumours that the Canadian government was planning to build a railway right through buffalo country. Settlers and railways would destroy buffalo hunting. Some Métis were ready to fight to keep what they believed was rightfully theirs. The Métis of the Red River Settlement gathered in a council meeting. They turned for leadership to a twenty-five-year-old Métis man, Louis Riel.

On 11 October 1869, the crew of Canadian surveyors stepped onto André Nault's land. Nault, a cousin of Louis Riel, saddled his horse and rode for help. He returned with Riel and sixteen Métis. Riel placed his foot on the surveyor's chain and said, "You go no farther." The Canadians left and reported the incident to Ottawa.

When Riel was asked why he had done this, he said that the Canadian government had no right to make surveys before the land had been transferred to Canada. With that act, Louis Riel stepped onto the stage of Canadian history and became the champion of the Métis people. The **Red River Rebellion** was about to begin.

The Red River Rebellion, 1869-70

One week after Louis Riel halted the work of the surveyors, he formed the **National Committee of the Métis**. The committee was to decide how to protect Métis lands. Shortly afterwards, the Métis heard that in preparation for the takeover of the Hudson's Bay lands, Ottawa had appointed William McDougall as the new Lieutenant-Governor. He was about to arrive at Fort Garry to govern the territory.

When McDougall arrived at the border of the settlement, he found the road to Fort Garry blocked by representatives of the National Committee of the Métis. They told him to return to Ottawa. They would not have any governor without being consulted first. McDougall had no choice. He turned back to the closest American frontier town and waited for orders from Ottawa.

In the meantime, Louis Riel and his followers captured the fortress of Fort Garry without firing a shot. They set up a government of their own to replace the Hudson's Bay Company's rule of the colony. Known as the **Provisional Government**, Riel said it would represent the area in any dealings with the Canadian government.

Some people in the settlement thought that this was an act of rebellion. But Riel never considered himself a rebel. His people were loyal citizens of the Queen. The Métis were fighting against two things. First, the Hudson's Bay Company had sold their land to Canada without telling them. Second, the Canadian government was taking over without consulting them.

People thought that Macdonald would

Fort Garry, 1863. The fort was the seat of government for the Hudson's Bay Company in Rupert's Land.

rush troops to the Red River to remove Riel from Fort Garry. But Macdonald chose another course. He was well aware that the Red River Settlement did not belong to Canada until 1 December 1869. Canada would not accept the region before there was peace.

The Thomas Scott Affair

Most of the people of the Red River Settlement supported Riel's government. Only a small group in the colony who had come from Ontario refused to accept it. They were known as "the Canadians." The Canadians showed little respect for the Métis people and refused to accept Riel's Provisional Government. One of these Canadians was Thomas Scott. When riots broke out, a number of Canadians, including Thomas Scott, were jailed by Riel.

The people of Red River drew up a **Métis Bill of Rights** and sent it to Ottawa. The major demands were as follows:

1. the territory must have the right to enter Canada's Confederation as a province;
2. they should be represented in Ottawa by four Members of Parliament and two senators;
3. they should have control over their local affairs;
4. French and English languages should be equal in schools and law courts;
5. the Métis should be able to keep their land, customs, and way of life.

These requests were considered fair in Ottawa. But then a serious incident occurred. Thomas Scott, who was in jail on a charge of taking up arms against Riel's government, struck his guards, called the Métis a pack of cowards, insulted their Roman Catholic religion, and threatened to murder Riel. Riel immediately ordered that Scott be brought to trial. The court found him guilty and demanded the death penalty. Within twenty-four hours, Thomas Scott was brought before a firing squad and executed.

Why did Riel allow such a sentence to be carried out so quickly? Riel may have wanted to prove to the Canadian government that he was in charge and meant business: "We wanted to be sure that our attitude was taken seriously," he later explained to a friend. Then Ottawa would have to work out the terms of the colony's entrance into Confederation with the Provisional Government. He also wanted to discourage the Canadians living in the settlement from stirring up more trouble.

When the news of Thomas Scott's execution reached Ontario, the uproar began. Feelings ran high as people in his home province were outraged by his death. Ontario was primarily English-speaking and Protestant. Newspapers throughout the province called for

An artist's view of Thomas Scott's execution. What impression does this picture give of the execution? Do you think it was drawn by a supporter or opponent of Riel?

revenge. People demanded that Riel be hanged for Scott's murder. They even offered a reward for Riel's arrest.

On the other hand, in the predominantly Roman Catholic province of Quebec, many thought Riel's actions were justified. They were sympathetic towards Riel and his government. They called him a hero and a defender of French rights. They placed the blame for the problem in the Red River Settlement on the "troublemakers" from Ontario.

The execution of Thomas Scott aroused bitter feelings between English and French Canadians. It would be a long time before the case of Thomas Scott was forgotten.

Aftermath of the Rebellion

Riel's Provisional Government worked out an agreement with Ottawa called the **Manitoba Act**. On 15 July 1870, the province of Manitoba entered Confederation. A small square of settled area around Fort Garry became Canada's fifth province. The rest of the former Hudson's Bay land was renamed the North-West Territories.

Riel was pleased with the Manitoba Act and proud that, under his leadership, they had founded a new province. The Manitoba Act set up the same system of government as in the other provinces. He had won the right to be represented in Ottawa with four seats in the House of Commons and two in the Senate. Like Quebec,

French and English in Manitoba had equal status. There would be French schools and protection for the French language and the Roman Catholic religion. The Métis had received about 560 000 ha of land for their use. However, many Métis soon became dissatisfied as more settlers moved into Manitoba. They moved farther west to join other Métis in the area of Canada we now know as Saskatchewan. They hoped to be able to hunt buffalo and follow their traditional way of life.

Meanwhile, Macdonald decided to send troops to the Red River in case of more trouble. The force was made up of British and Canadian troops headed by Colonel Garnet Wolseley. A military force in Manitoba would also send a clear signal to the United States that Canada was laying claim to the West.

It took thirteen weeks for Colonel Wolseley to reach Manitoba. Since there was no railway, the soldiers often had to build a road as they went along. As they neared Winnipeg, Riel began to fear that

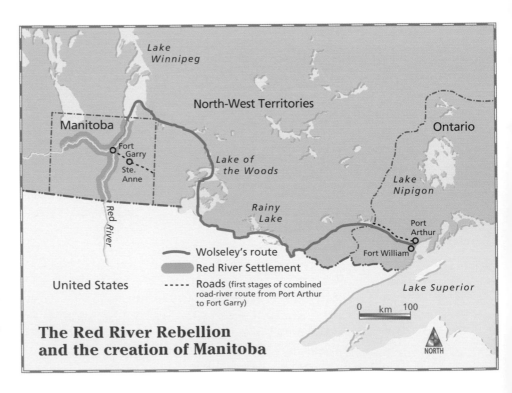

The Red River Rebellion and the creation of Manitoba

Louis Riel and his council

he might be seized and punished for the death of Thomas Scott. His followers begged him to flee. Riel escaped on horseback and rode off to the United States. It would be fifteen years before the Métis would see their leader again.

British Columbia Considers Confederation

British Columbians had different ideas about the future of their colony. The united colony of British Columbia was far from strong. The end of the gold rush and the decline of the fur trade had left the economy depressed. The population of 40 000 consisted of an estimated 30 000 aboriginal peoples. There were a few well established communities, such as Victoria with a population of 4000 people, the coal-mining area of Nanaimo with 700 people, and New Westminster with over 1000 people. The rest of the population was scattered over the vast, rugged, and largely uninhabited areas of the province.

A small group of influential people, mainly officials of the Hudson's Bay Company and some government leaders, favoured remaining as a crown colony with a governor and a representative government. Another group thought the colony should join the American Northwest. These were mainly business people who were encouraged by Americans who wanted to annex British Columbia.

A third group promoted the idea of union with the Dominion of Canada. De Cosmos was one of the most active supporters of joining the Canadian Confederation. He used his newspaper, *The British Colonist*, to advance this cause. In September 1869, De Cosmos organized a convention at Yale where resolutions were passed for union with Canada and responsible government. The officials of the colony and the Hudson's Bay Company immediately denounced the convention and called it treason. The people who favoured annexation sent a petition with 104 signatures to US President Ulysses S. Grant asking that British Columbia be allowed to join the

United States. The work of those who opposed annexation helped to build wider support for union with Canada. The British government also favoured British Columbia's entry into the Dominion. When Britain appointed a new governor he was instructed to encourage the colony's entry into Confederation.

Terms of British Columbia's Entry into Confederation

On 10 May 1870, three delegates left Victoria for Ottawa to discuss suitable terms for the colony's entry into Confederation. They were John Sebastian Helmcken, Dr. R.W. Carrall of the Cariboo, and Joseph Trutch, who had helped to build the Cariboo Road. The delegates travelled by steamer to San Francisco, and by rail to Ottawa. It took them twenty-three days to reach the capital. They told Macdonald that British Columbia was interested in joining Confederation. They asked for responsible government, just as the other provinces had. Responsible government meant that if the people became unhappy with the politicians, they could be voted out of office. The British Columbians also wanted Canada to build a wagon road across the prairies and through the mountains to link British Columbia to the East. They wanted the federal government to take over the provincial debt of over $1 000 000 and to begin a road-building campaign.

The delegates were welcomed in Ottawa with even better terms than they had asked for. Prime Minister John A. Macdonald was ill, so George-Étienne Cartier handled the negotiations. British Columbia was offered a railway, not a wagon road, across the prairies and through the mountains to link British Columbia to the East. It was to be started within two years and completed within ten. British Columbia would receive full provincial status, an annual subsidy of $35 000, and a yearly per capita grant of

Celebrations as British Columbia enters Confederation

Charlottetown, PEI, at the time of joining Confederation

80¢ until the population reached 400 000. The federal government also assumed the new province's debt.

It had been Macdonald's dream to link Canada to the Pacific Ocean, "a Dominion from sea to sea." The new province would be joined to the rest of Canada by a ribbon of steel. British Columbia would also provide Canada with extensive natural resources such as gold and lumber. On 20 July 1871, British Columbia entered the Dominion of Canada.

Aboriginal Peoples and the New Province

Although British Columbia was almost as large as the original Dominion of Canada, only an estimated 43 000 people lived there at the time of the province's entry into Confederation. It is estimated that 33 000 of these inhabitants were aboriginal peoples. No one asked them how they liked the idea of joining Canada. Aboriginal peoples did not become citizens of the Dominion with the right to vote. It was not until 1960 that they got the right to vote in federal elections. In British Columbia, they received the right to vote in provincial elections in 1949.

Life was particularly difficult for aboriginal peoples. Almost 35 per cent of the population had died during the smallpox epidemics that broke out during the gold rush years. The decline of the fur trade and the expansion of settlement also helped to destroy the traditional ways of life. No treaties were signed between Canada and the aboriginal peoples of British Columbia, as had been signed east of the Rockies. Aboriginal peoples were eventually reduced to living on small reserves. The government tried to discourage the preservation of their languages and traditions. For example, in 1884 the potlatch ceremony was banned by the federal government. For some time the potlatch was practised in secret. But in the 1920s a number of arrests were made, with police seizing masks and other objects used in the ceremony. Not until 1951 was the ban removed.

Prince Edward Island Joins Confederation

In 1867, Prince Edward Island had turned Confederation down flat. During the next six years, however, Islanders began to have second thoughts.

By 1873, Prince Edward Island was deeply in debt trying to build a railway. When the people of the island learned that they would have to pay higher taxes or join Confederation, the prospect of joining Canada began to appear good. For its part, Canada still wanted Prince Edward Island within Confederation. As long as it remained outside, Prince Edward Island could be used as an American base for an attack on Canada.

On 1 July 1873, Prince Edward Island joined Confederation. By the terms of the agreement, Canada provided $800 000 to buy the land on the island from the absentee landlords. Canada also took over the province's debts, including those caused by the new railway. It promised, too, that there would be a year-round ferry boat service from the mainland to the island, as well as a telegraph service.

DEVELOPING SKILLS: DEBATING

Do you ever get involved in heated arguments with your family or friends? Are you determined to convince them that your point of view is right? Then you will enjoy debating! A debate is a formal discussion during which points of view for and against an issue are presented. You probably debate more often than you think, although usually informally. Can you remember your last discussion with your parents over whether or not you should be grounded? What arguments were presented on both sides?

You may also have seen formal debates between politicians or journalists on television. Members of Parliament in government also debate key issues before a bill is passed. Lawyers use debating skills in the courtroom. But in almost any career or occupation, you can benefit from knowing how to prepare an argument and present it effectively.

Most formal debates begin with a presentation of the issue in the form of a clear statement. For example, "The Métis in the Red River in 1869 were justified in doing what they did." Two teams are then set up. One team, the "pro" side, presents arguments in favour of the statement. The other team, the "con" side, presents arguments against the statement. Counterarguments are then heard. The goal is to reach a decision on the issue after careful consideration of all of the arguments and counterarguments on both sides.

There are many issues related to the opening of the West that have sparked heated debate over the years. In your class, decide on one of the following issues to debate:

- "British Columbians would not enter Confederation if the decision were being made today."
- "Louis Riel deserves the title Founder of Manitoba."

■ Step 1: Preparation

1. Divide the class into two groups. One group represents the "pro" side and the other the "con" side.
2. Research your topic thoroughly. Make sure you separate facts from opinions.

3. Organize your information so that you have reasoned arguments to support your side in the debate. Support your opinions with facts. Use statements by experts on your topic.

4. With your teammates, develop a game plan so that everyone knows his or her role. Remember that every team member must prepare and participate equally.

5. Practise your delivery at home or with other members of your team. Have your teammates suggest ways to improve your presentation.

6. Try to anticipate the arguments of your opponents and have some counterarguments prepared.

■ Step 2: Process

7. When you are ready for the debate, choose three people to speak for your side. One student in the class acts as the moderator. The moderator's job is to ensure that the debate flows smoothly and that emotions don't get out of control.

8. The speakers for the two teams then present their arguments in turn, beginning with the leader of the "pro" team, followed by the leader of the "con" team, and so on. Each speaker adds arguments for his or her side and attempts to counter the arguments of the previous speaker from the opposing side.

9. The concluding speaker for each side should summarize the major arguments for his or her team.

■ Step 3: Follow-up

10. After the debate, have a class vote on which team had the most convincing arguments. Your vote should be based on the debaters' skills, not on whether you agree with their position. Follow up with a class discussion on why the arguments were strong or weak. Class members may suggest arguments that were left out in the debate or refute points raised by either team.

The Dream of a Railway

John A. Macdonald had a dream to link Canada's east and west coasts with a ribbon of steel. British Columbia had joined Canada on the promise that a railway would be built. But a railway had other advantages as well. It would encourage westward expansion and settlement by moving settlers west and bringing their farm products to eastern markets.

But what a task a transcontinental railway was! Surveyors were required to find the best route through swamps, forests, mountains, and plains. Expert engineers

The government wanted to build a railway across the country to the Pacific to encourage westward expansion and settlement.

were needed to build bridges and blast tunnels. Thousands of labourers would have to perform the back-breaking work of putting down track. But above all else, it would cost a lot of money.

A group of business people led by Sir Hugh Allan formed the **Pacific Railway Company** to do the job. But the plan soon collapsed as it was revealed that Allan and his friends had given large amounts of money to Macdonald's government. It looked as if Allan had bribed the government for the right to build the railway. The event became known as the **Pacific Scandal** and it forced Macdonald and the Conservatives to resign in 1873. It appeared that the railway would never be built and that Sir John A. Macdonald, a founder of Confederation, would end his career in disgrace.

For the next five years, the Liberal party formed the government of Canada. Alexander Mackenzie was the country's second prime minister. The Liberals had never been enthusiastic about pouring large amounts of money into the railway. They thought that the scheme was far too expensive for such a young country. Instead, the Liberals decided to build the railway bit by bit whenever the country could afford it.

The National Policy and the CPR

In the election of 1878, however, Macdonald was returned to power. The Conservatives had put forward a **National Policy** to solve the country's economic problems. They wanted to keep cheaper American goods out of Canada and to encourage Canadians to buy goods made by Canadians. They also wanted to fill the rich prairie lands with settlers, who would be encouraged to buy manufactured goods made in

An election poster supporting Macdonald's National Policy

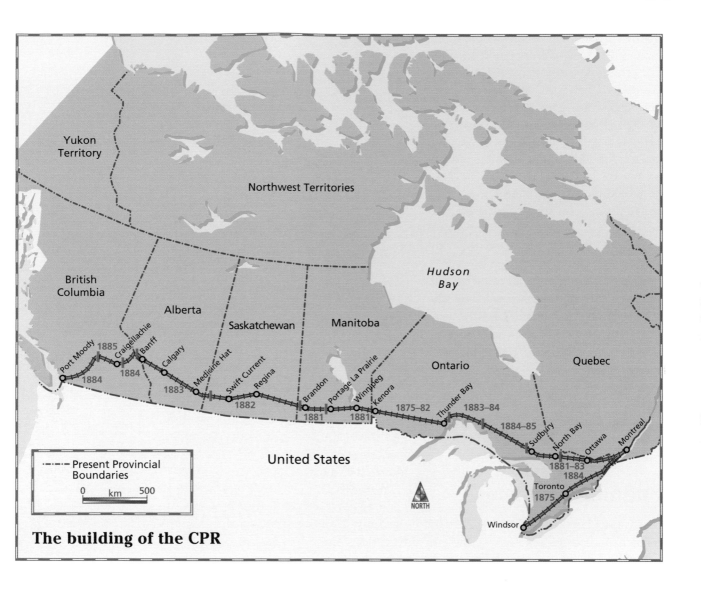

Yukon
Territory

Northwest Territories

British
Columbia

Hudson
Bay

Alberta

Saskatchewan

Manitoba

Port Moody 1885
Craigellachie
Banff
Calgary
Medicine Hat
Swift Current
Regina
Brandon
Portage La Prairie
Winnipeg
Kenora
Thunder Bay

Ontario

Quebec

1884
1884
1883
1882
1881
1881
1875–82
1883–84

1884–85

Sudbury
North Bay
Ottawa
Montreal

United States

1881–83
1884

Toronto
1875

Windsor

-·-·- Present Provincial
Boundaries

0   km   500

NORTH

The building of the CPR

eastern Canada and to sell their agricultural products to eastern Canadians. But to make all this possible, an east-west transcontinental railway had to be built.

Not all Canadians supported the National Policy, however. The policy encouraged an east-west economy. Natural resources flowed into central Canada and manufactured goods flowed out. One problem was that many of the provinces produced the same goods. The Atlantic provinces, in particular, opposed the National Policy. It made more sense

to trade north-south with the United States, and there was a long history of trade between the Maritime provinces and their southern neighbour. It was cheaper to transport goods south than across the vast distances to central Canada.

With the National Policy in place, the railway project was on again! In 1880, George Stephen and Donald A. Smith headed the newly formed **Canadian Pacific Railway Company**. Stephen and Smith worked out a deal with Macdonald's Conservative government. In return for building the railway, the company would own and operate it. In addition, the government would give the company 10 million hectares of land. This land would later be sold to settlers to raise money for the company. The 1100 km of railway lines that had already been finished would also be transferred to the Canadian Pacific Railway Company.

The Conservative government granted the company a twenty-year **monopoly**. This meant that the Canadian Pacific would have complete control of all east-west rail traffic in the southern part of the prairies for twenty years. All materials needed for the railway, such as steel tracks and spikes, could be brought into Canada tax-free. All Canadian Pacific stations, sidings, and lands were to be tax-free forever. In return, the railway company promised to complete the line to British Columbia within ten years. About 3040 km of track were yet to be built.

Building Problems

The Canadian Pacific Railway hired William Van Horne to supervise the construction process. Canadian geography presented gigantic problems for Van Horne and the construction crew. On the flat, open prairies it was fairly easy to lay track. But in northern Ontario and the Rockies, it was quite a different matter! Van Horne's idea was to start work at different places. One team started to build the railway in northern Ontario and worked towards Winnipeg. Other gangs started building from the Pacific coast, and from Winnipeg towards the mountains. In the mountains, teams were building both east and west. Van Horne made sure that the building operation was run as efficiently as an army.

When Van Horne first saw the region north of Lake Superior he called it "two

William Van Horne

hundred miles of engineering impossibility." His workers had to cut down hills, fill in swamps, blast through hard granite, and lower the levels of lakes. To make matters worse, they were driven mad by mosquitoes day and night!

Northern Ontario rock was a major challenge. It took $7.5 million worth of dynamite to move the Ontario granite. North of Lake Superior, nitroglycerine was used daily. This explosive was so dangerous that it could not be carried in wagons. Labourers had to carry it in bottles strapped to their backs. A stumble or fall meant certain death. In one stretch of 80 km, more than thirty workers lost their lives! They were killed by explosions or falling rocks. This was the human cost of building Canada's transcontinental railway.

The Challenge of Crossing the Mountains

The British Columbia section of the railway was the most difficult and dangerous. The mountains had to be crossed.

UNREST AMONG ABORIGINAL PEOPLES

Crowfoot, Father Lacombe, and Three Bulls

The path of the railway caused unrest among aboriginal peoples. A serious incident arose with Crowfoot and the Blackfoot. They had signed a treaty with the Canadian government in 1877 that had forced them to give up their land and move onto a reserve. They were told that no other people could trespass on the reserve. But the railway began to move onto the corner of the Blackfoot reservation.

The Blackfoot were angry and insulted that they had not been advised of the railway's plans. They felt that they were being tricked by the government and the railway company. They were ready to try to drive the builders off their land. Father Lacombe, a missionary who was close to the Blackfoot, urged caution. He persuaded the Blackfoot Council to allow the railway to use a small piece of their land. He promised that in return the government would give them extra land. The Blackfoot listened to Lacombe's advice and the crisis passed.

Wooden trestles had to be built over deep river canyons. A **trestle** is a framework used as a bridge to support the railway tracks. The Mountain Creek trestle was 50 m high and 331 m long. It looked so fragile that one engineer refused to drive his engine over it. Van Horne threatened to take over the controls himself. Then the red-faced engineer replied, "If you ain't afraid of getting killed Mr. Van Horne, with all your money, I ain't afraid either." Van Horne answered, "We'll have a double funeral—at my expense of course." The engine passed over the trestle safely.

In places, the railway was forced to creep along the edges of cliffs. Below, torrents and rapids roared. One of the most terrifying stretches of trail was a narrow ledge, less than 60 cm wide. All supplies had to be brought along that trail. It was so frightening that the labourers used to hang onto the tails of their pack horses to get across. Some kept their eyes shut until they had passed through the most dangerous places!

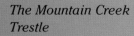

The Mountain Creek Trestle

In many places, workers had to blast a way for the tracks through the rocks. They had to be lowered on ropes down the slippery canyon walls, barefoot so they could keep their balance better. They drilled holes in the rock for the dynamite charges. Then they were hauled back up to the surface and everyone ran for cover. Many workers died or were injured by pieces of flying rock. The work was so dangerous that some claimed "every kilometre of tunnel and track was stained with blood along the British Columbia section of the line."

CHARACTERS IN CANADIAN HISTORY: CHINESE RAILWAY WORKERS

To keep costs down, several thousand Chinese workers were brought into the country to work on the British Columbia stretch of the railway. These men, who were mostly landless peasants, had to leave their wives and children behind in China. Their goal was to save enough money working in North America, in the land they called the *Gum San*—the Golden Mountain—to return to China and buy a small plot of land. They were willing to work hard for half the wages other workers expected.

Separate camps were set up for the Chinese workers. Rice, salmon, and tea were the main staples of their diets. Many became sick from scurvy, a disease caused by a lack of fresh vegetables. Since there were no doctors, many workers died in the camps.

Chinese workers labour on the railway in British Columbia. The Chinese played an important role in the construction of the CPR.

The Chinese workers were often badly treated. Some citizens of British Columbia objected to the Chinese because they appeared different. Their clothing, language, hairstyle, customs, and skin colour set them apart. They were accused of taking jobs away from other workers. But the railway company could never find enough workers willing to do backbreaking labour for such low wages. Railway officials often gave the Chinese workers the most dangerous jobs. Many men fell to their deaths pulling supplies up the treacherous Fraser River. Others lost their lives in blasting accidents and rockslides. No wonder it is said that, without Chinese labourers, British Columbia would not have had a railway.

Few of the Chinese workers ever saved enough money to return to their families in China. Though each Chinese worker was paid about $25 a month, most of this was deducted for room and board. When the construction jobs ended, most Chinese workers had no choice but to stay in Canada. They faced a grim future in a country where they seemed unwanted. To survive, many took low-paying jobs that other people found disagreeable.

Over the years, Chinese-Canadians have contributed to the country's prosperity. They launched the market garden industry in British Columbia and established thousands of businesses across the country. They have worked in many professions and have become prominent citizens of Canada.

The Last Spike!

The last railway spike was driven at 9:22 a.m. on 7 November 1885. The brief ceremony marking the completion of the railway took place high in the Eagle Pass at Craigellachie, British Columbia. Donald Smith drove in an iron spike and at last Montreal and the Pacific were linked by a ribbon of steel. The contract allowed the company ten years to build the railway. It was completed in five.

What did the completion of the CPR mean for Canada? First, it meant that one of British Columbia's conditions for joining Confederation had been honoured. Now the province was linked to Canada. The United States could not take over the whole Pacific Coast. The new railway also made it easier for people to settle in western Canada. As farm populations increased, communities would grow around them. Finally, movement was now faster and easier between the west and east coasts. This would encourage trade within the country rather than with the United States.

After a trip of 139 hours, the first passenger train arrived in Port Moodie, British Columbia, on 4 July 1886. The Pacific Express was only one minute late.

DEVELOPING SKILLS: MAKING ORAL PRESENTATIONS

Are you someone who prefers to talk about a subject rather than write about it? Oral presentations can allow you to use your skills. Even if you feel nervous about talking in front of a group, some basic steps can help you feel comfortable and set you on the road to presenting an interesting and informative talk.

Oral presentations are an important skill. In many careers and occupations, you will need to give informed talks on some aspect of your work. Lawyers, salespeople, journalists, sportscasters, tradespeople, teachers, artists, and many others use speaking skills every day. You probably already use speaking skills more often than you think. When you talk about your hobbies, help friends with homework, or explain a new computer game, you are using some oral presentation skills.

The key to good oral presentations is practice. The more often you do them, the more comfortable you feel and the better your presentations become. Don't worry about making mistakes or sounding foolish. If you are prepared and enthusiastic, you deserve your audience's attention. Here are some helpful steps.

■ Step 1: Plan

1. Make sure you understand the topic. Ask questions if there is anything you aren't sure about. Know when you will present and how much time you have.
2. Make a written plan of the full presentation, just as you would for a written report. Put the main ideas and subpoints in your own words. The presentation should have:
   a) an introduction that states the main theme, issue, or purpose of the presentation. Try to make the opening powerful to catch the attention and interest of your audience. Consider using a personal reference, a thoughtful question, a startling statistic, a quotation, or a visual such as a slide or picture. For example, one student started a presentation this way:

   One of my ancestors arrived in Vancouver from China in the 1880s. He was one of thousands of labourers who came from China to help build the CPR. All he had with him was a small bundle of clothes and a few coins of money.

   b) content that includes ideas and facts to support your main theme.
   c) illustrations to clarify ideas and support your arguments. Your audience will find your presentation more interesting if you use examples and visuals to prove your points. You could use charts, pictures, slides, video clips, tape recordings, or quotes.
   d) a clear, logical organization. Follow a written plan. Deal with one subtopic at a time. Arrange your ideas in a logical sequence. This will help your audience focus on your theme and follow your thinking. For example, an oral presentation on Chinese railway workers could ask and then answer each of the following questions:
   • Who were the Chinese labourers?
   • Why did they come to Canada?
   • What did their job involve?
   • What were some of the problems they had in adjusting to their new lives?
   • What happened to them when the railway was completed?
   e) a summary that reinforces your message and sums up what you have been showing. You may want to end with a powerful anecdote, quotation, or even a thought-provoking question. A sample summary might be:

   My ancestor never saved enough to return to China. He and the other Chinese were not always treated kindly in British Columbia. Many, however, like my ancestor, eventually built a new life here and grew to love their adopted country. He always spoke proudly of the important part he had played in bringing the railway into British Columbia.

■ Step 2: Rehearse

3. Practise from your script, but try not to read your notes.

4. Rehearse out loud in front of a mirror. Use gestures that come to you naturally as you talk and try to keep eye contact with your audience.

5. Vary the volume and pace of your presentation, just as you would in a conversation about something that interests you. Using visuals at key points in your presentation can help vary the pace. Listen to yourself on tape.

6. Rehearse over and over until you are comfortable with your material and don't have to read from your notes.

7. Time your practice. Be sure to leave time for questions and discussion. Be ready for questions.

■ Step 3: Deliver

8. Sit or stand straight and keep eye contact with your audience so that they feel you are talking to them personally.

9. Show enthusiasm for your topic. If you enjoy it, your audience will too. It's catching!

10. Have members of the class make notes during the presentation. This encourages them to listen carefully. Check with your teacher about this.

11. Have an outline or brief notes to refer to occasionally, but don't read from your notes. Mark off new points with a pause or vocal change. Repeat key points for emphasis but avoid repetition of certain words or phrases. Use simple language and explain difficult terms. Use language your audience understands.

12. Speak clearly and distinctly and make sure you can be heard. The presentation will lose a lot of its appeal if you cannot be heard or understood.

Now that you know the steps, practise them. Research and prepare an oral presentation on one of the following topics on building the CPR:

• The Chinese railway workers
• Mapping the route for the CPR
• Preparing the roadbed and laying the track
• The challenge of building through the mountains
• Life in a railroad camp
• Political and railway company personalties
• The last spike ceremony
• The effects of the railway on aboriginal peoples

ACTIVITIES

Check Your Understanding

1. Add these new terms to your *Factfile*.

   • Rupert's Land • North-West Territories • Métis • Red River Rebellion • National Committee of the Métis • Provisional Government • Métis Bill of Rights • Manitoba Act • Pacific Railway Company • Pacific Scandal • National Policy • Canadian Pacific Railway Company • monopoly

2. a) Why did Canada want to buy the Hudson's Bay Company lands?
   b) Why did the Hudson's Bay Company want to keep some of its land instead of turning it over to Canada?

3. Imagine you are a Métis sent to Ottawa from the Red River Settlement. Make a list for the government of the problems faced by your people in 1869.

4. Describe the Thomas Scott affair. How did it arouse bitter feelings between French and English Canadians?

5. a) Why did Macdonald introduce the National Policy? What did its supporters claim it would do?
   b) How did Canadians react to the National Policy?

6. Use a comparison organizer to outline the advantages and disadvantages of the three options considered by British Columbians in the mid-1860s about the future of their colony.

7. In a chart, list the terms asked for and the terms received by British Columbia for entering Confederation.

8. Describe the problems faced by the aboriginal peoples of British Columbia at the time of the province's entry into Confederation.

9. Describe the problems of building the railway through northern Ontario and British Columbia. What were the solutions to these problems? What were the costs?

Confirm Your Learning

10. Did these new provinces—Manitoba, British Columbia, and Prince Edward Island—get a fair deal when they entered Confederation? Why or why not? Explain your view.

11. a) In an organizer, compare the terms asked for by the Métis and those asked for by British Columbia on entering Confederation.
    b) In what ways were the requests similar?
    c) Were the Métis asking for anything special? Explain.

12. Explain how each of the following factors affected the building of the railway in Canada:
    a) climate
    b) physical landforms
    c) money
    d) personalities (Van Horne, Stephen, Macdonald)
    e) labourers.

13. List some of the difficulties that the Chinese railway workers faced in Canada. Why do you think Chinese workers were not treated as well as Canadian workers and workers from other countries?

14. Why do you think the Canadian government failed to negotiate with the Blackfoot for the land they needed for the CPR? What does this incident tell you about relations between aboriginal peoples and the government in the early days of the West?

Challenge Your Mind

15. Review the material in Chapter 1 about the meaning of the word **rebellion**, then answer the following questions. Be prepared to support your answers.

a) Who would Riel and the Métis say was the established government in the Red River Settlement in November 1869? Explain.

b) Who would Macdonald say was the established government in the settlement at this time? Explain.

c) Can we call the situation in the Red River in 1869 a rebellion? Why or why not?

16. Discuss this statement: "Without the railway, there would not have been the country of Canada from sea to sea."

17. Debate: "The completion of the CPR was as important an event in Canadian history as Confederation."

18. Read the following passage about Canada's immigration policy between 1895 and 1947, then answer the questions that follow:

> *Between 1895 and 1947, laws were passed in Canada to keep Chinese people out. These were brought about largely by pressure from unions of workers. The workers were afraid the Chinese might take away their jobs.*
>
> *A tax of $50 had to be paid by each Chinese person wishing to enter Canada. In 1900, this tax was raised to $100, and in 1903 to $500.*
>
> *The Chinese Immigration Act of 1923 said that no Chinese people were allowed to enter Canada unless they were merchants or students. Between 1923 and 1947, only forty-four Chinese people were allowed into Canada.*

a) What do you think were the reasons for not admitting Chinese people to Canada? Do you think that these reasons were fair? Why or why not?

b) How effective do you think the tax was in keeping Chinese people out? Explain your answer.

c) Do you think the Chinese Immigration Act was an example of racial discrimination? Explain your answer.

A certificate showing the payment of the $500 head tax by a Chinese immigrant

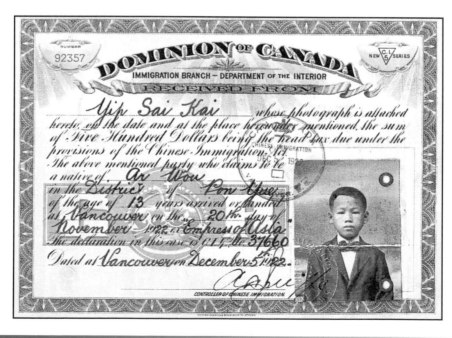

CHAPTER 5

Preparing the West for Settlement

MASSACRE!

1 June 1873   Cypress Hills, NWT

American wolf hunters today attacked a band of Assiniboine Indians in the Cypress Hills. An American "wolfer" falsely accused Chief Little Soldier's people of stealing a horse in Montana. The Americans came north looking for revenge. The "wolfers" burst into the aboriginal camp, killing thirty-six men, women, and children. It turned out that the missing horse had just wandered away.

Even before this incident, aboriginal peoples resented the American wolf hunters. These wolfers use strychnine to poison their bait, but the bait is often eaten by aboriginal people's dogs, which then die agonizing deaths. The American traders also bring another kind of poison—cheap liquor known as "firewater," which they sell to the aboriginal people.

Because of incidents like the Cypress Hills Massacre, the Canadian government will be forced to act. Sooner or later, Macdonald will have to find a way to establish law and order if he wants to prepare the North-West for settlement.

The Need for Police

For years, people in the North-West had complained about the outlaws and illegal whisky traders in the area. It was against the law to sell alcohol, but there was no police force in the region to enforce the law. A place nicknamed Fort Whoop-Up, near the present-day city of Lethbridge, Alberta, was the centre of this outlaw activity. The people who lived there were mostly American smugglers and traders who even flew the American flag over the fort.

The situation in the West was becoming desperate. In 1874, Parliament decided to form the **North-West Mounted Police**. The duties of the force were to keep peace, prevent crime, and catch criminals. It would be a mounted force and a chain of posts would be built from Manitoba to the Rocky Mountains.

Recruiting began at once in the towns and cities in eastern Canada. Although the pay was only a dollar a day with free room and board, there was no shortage of recruits. Young people seeking adventure flocked to join the force. By the summer of 1874, 300 recruits were gathered in Manitoba to be sworn in as Mounties.

The new force was faced with an almost impossible task. It had to look after 6 million square kilometres and thousands of people with a force of only 300 police. Once permanent police posts were established in the West, the real work of the Mounties could begin. First, the liquor trade had to be controlled and stopped. Some whisky traders were taking furs in exchange for a powerful drink called "Whoop-Up Bug Juice." Whoop-Up Bug Juice was made by colouring alcohol with black chewing tobacco and spiking it with red pepper and ginger. This "firewater" was sold to aboriginal peoples at outrageous prices. One buffalo robe bought only twenty cups.

The Mounties were determined to bring the whisky trade to an end. Traders were caught and fined and their whisky

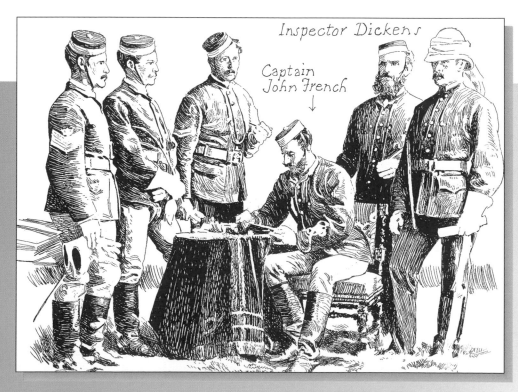

The North-West Mounted Police, 1874

was poured on the ground. Within a short time, most of the whisky traders were run out of "Whoop-Up country" and law and order were being established.

The Mounties also had to win the respect of the aboriginal peoples. They told them that the Redcoats had not come to take away the land but to drive out the whisky traders and bring law and justice to the West. All people were to be treated the same under the law. Many aboriginal chiefs welcomed the Mounties and grew to trust them.

This friendship was tested in May 1876. A messenger from Sitting Bull, chief of the American Sioux, was sent to the Blackfoot camp. The Sioux had fought American cavalry at the famous battle at Little Bighorn to protest against the settlers and prospectors who had taken over their hunting grounds. Sitting Bull invited Crowfoot and the Blackfoot to join the Sioux in war against both the American soldiers and the Canadian Mounties. Some of the Blackfoot called for war. But Crowfoot reminded them that the Mounties were friends. The police had driven out the whisky traders and jailed the wolfers who had killed their people. Crowfoot refused to join the Sioux.

In the 1870s and 1880s, the Canadian government made treaties with some aboriginal peoples that moved them onto reserves. In Canada, unlike in the United States, this was achieved with only a few incidents of violence. In part, this was due to the friendship between the aboriginal peoples and the Mounties. Disillusionment on the part of aboriginal peoples came later.

Blackfoot chiefs meet with the Mounties

The Need for Treaties

After Confederation, the Canadian government wanted to open western lands for settlement. To do so, government agents had to persuade **First Nations** peoples to sign treaties and move onto reserves. A **treaty** is an agreement between parties or nations for the purchase or transfer of land or property. **Reserves** were lands set aside for aboriginal peoples on which they would have special rights. Others would not be able to hunt, fish, or settle on these reserve lands.

Canada Makes Treaties

Following Confederation, aboriginal peoples became the most regulated people in Canada. In 1876, the Canadian government introduced the **Indian Act**, which introduced even more regulations. Traditional ceremonies, such as the potlatch, were banned. It was decided that aboriginal children must attend special residential schools. The government required aboriginal peoples to give up their nomadic lifestyle and move onto reserves and become farmers.

But the aboriginal peoples did not want to be controlled in this way. They had lived their nomadic life of hunting, trapping, and fishing for centuries. They had no experience in farming, nor did they want to be farmers. What they wanted was to keep their independence. They felt they should have the right to maintain their culture, languages, and way of life. But the signing of the treaties made this difficult. Why, then, did they sign?

Aboriginal groups on the prairies faced a crisis. For centuries, their way of life had been based on the buffalo. The buffalo provided their food, clothing, and most other necessities of life. But by the 1870s, the vast buffalo herds were disappearing from the plains. Settlers and ranchers were hunting buffalo for sport. The demand for buffalo robes and tongues encouraged ruthless slaughter of these animals. It was not unusual to find hundreds of buffalo bodies rotting on the prairies, with only their tongues and hides removed. In less than ten years, the buffalo herds were almost wiped out. Buffalo bones scattered across the land were all that remained of the massive herds that had once roamed the plains.

This changed the way of life of the aboriginal peoples forever. With the buffalo gone, they were facing starvation. The government said that farming on reserve lands would provide them with a source of food. The soil on many reserves, however, was often poor and unproductive.

A second disaster also struck about this time. When Europeans came to Canada, they brought diseases such as measles, tuberculosis, and smallpox. Since these diseases were new to North America, aboriginal peoples had no natural resistance, and their traditional medicines were defenceless against them. In the smallpox epidemic of 1870, about 800 members of the Blackfoot population died. Disease and death severely

For the aboriginal peoples of the Plains, hunting buffalo was an important part of their livelihood.

lowered the spirits of the aboriginal peoples.

In addition, settlers were pouring into the West. Now that the North-West Mounted Police were established, people felt it was safe to settle there. As the railway moved farther west, more and more settlers arrived. Towns such as Calgary, Medicine Hat, Swift Current, Regina, and Moose Jaw developed along the railway's path. Aboriginal peoples were in a difficult situation. In the United States, aboriginal groups were fighting a losing battle against the settlers. Their lands were being taken and many aboriginal people were being killed by American soldiers and settlers. Facing starvation, devastating diseases, and increasing settlement, the proud nations of the plains felt they had no choice. They signed a series of treaties and moved onto reservations.

In Canada, eleven treaties were signed between the government and First Nations peoples of the plains between 1871 and 1921. These were the so-called **numbered treaties**. Over 2 million square kilometres were turned over to Canada by the terms of these treaties.

The northeast corner of British Columbia was part of Treaty No 8. This treaty was signed with the Beaver, Cree, and Slavey people. But other than this, no post-Confederation numbered treaties were signed in British Columbia.

Did aboriginal peoples believe they were giving up the land forever? Most aboriginal people say no. To them, land is like the air, the sky, and the water. It cannot be owned by any one person or group. It is part of nature, to be shared with all living things. Aboriginal peoples

The signing of the first treaty between the Canadian government and the Cree and Ojibway of southern Manitoba, 1871

believed they were making a friendship agreement—an agreement to share the land with other people as they shared it with the animals. The buffalo were disappearing. Settlers were coming into the area. Aboriginal leaders saw the treaties as a way of ensuring help and protection for their people in the future. In return for sharing the land, the government was to provide food, clothing, medicine, and money to help them establish a new way of life.

Treaties Bring Change

Adjustment to life on the reserves was difficult. For many aboriginal peoples, the treaties were "broken promises." Government food supplies often did not arrive, or there were not enough rations to go around. The government **agents**, placed as administrators on the reserves, sometimes cheated the people and treated them harshly. It is not surprising that some aboriginal people under chiefs Poundmaker and Big Bear grew discontented and rebellious.

CHARACTERS IN CANADIAN HISTORY: CROWFOOT, CHIEF OF THE BLACKFOOT

Chief Crowfoot

Crowfoot was born in 1830 as a member of the Blood. He became a Blackfoot when his widowed mother married a Blackfoot man. As a boy, he learned to ride and hunt. As a youth, he became known for courage. There is a story of how Crowfoot showed great bravery during a raid in Montana. The Blackfoot noticed one of their captured painted tipis in a Crow camp. "Whoever strikes that tipi," declared the Chief, "will be a future leader of our people." Crowfoot rushed towards the camp. The Crows saw him approach and fired on him. A bullet struck him in the arm but passed through, missing the bone. He stumbled for a moment, but got back up and raced on towards the painted tipi. He struck it with his whip, then fell to the ground. After this daring deed, he announced that he would take the honoured name of a brave ancestor. The name meant "Crow Indian's Big Foot," which interpreters shortened to Crowfoot. After that incident, many Blackfoot youths competed with one another for the right to join Crowfoot. By the early 1870s, Crowfoot had become a major chief of the Blackfoot.

As a chief, Crowfoot became a peacemaker. There was a long tradition of conflict between the Blackfoot and the Cree. To try to end it, Crowfoot adopted the Cree Chief Poundmaker as his own son.

Crowfoot also worked for peace between aboriginal peoples and settlers. He welcomed the North-West Mounted Police when they came to end the whisky trade. In the interest of his people's welfare, he signed Treaty No. 7 with the government. He used all his influence as a speaker and leader to keep the Blackfoot out of the North-West Rebellion in 1885.

Crowfoot was leader of the Blackfoot during distressing times. The buffalo had disappeared. Many Blackfoot were sick or starving. The government was pressing aboriginal peoples to sign treaties. The Blackfoot then had to adjust to life on reserves. Perhaps Crowfoot's most important contribution was helping his people to adapt to the new way of life.

Other Aboriginal Land Claims

About half of Canada's aboriginal peoples are not covered by treaties. Most of the aboriginal groups of British Columbia, Quebec, and the Northwest Territories have never transferred their lands to the government. As the descendants of the first inhabitants of that land, they believe they have rights to it because it has never been given up or extinguished by treaty. These are known as their **aboriginal rights**. They are demanding that the government settle their claim to the land and pay for the right to use it. Before hydroelectric plants or pipelines can be built, aboriginal peoples insist that the government assure them that they will receive a large share of the benefits from the land's development. As the original inhabitants of the land, they maintain that these claims are fair, just, and lawful. In some cases, they are taking their claims to the Supreme Court of Canada to prove it.

During the 1980s, aboriginal peoples challenged Canada to honour its promises to them. A new generation of political leaders emerged to carry on discussions with federal and provincial governments to regain lands held by their ancestors. The Haida and the Nisga'a of British Columbia, the Anishnabe of Ontario, the Lubicon of Alberta, and many other aboriginal groups have defended their land from miners, loggers, and developers. They have demanded that their rights be respected.

While some progress is being made, the struggle is a long one and it is far from complete. In April 1990, the largest land claim in Canada was settled. It gave the Inuit 350 000 km² of territory in the north. When it comes into effect on 1 April 1999, the new territory will be called Nunavut.

Not all land claims have been peaceful, however. In the summer of 1990, a land dispute resulted in an armed stand-

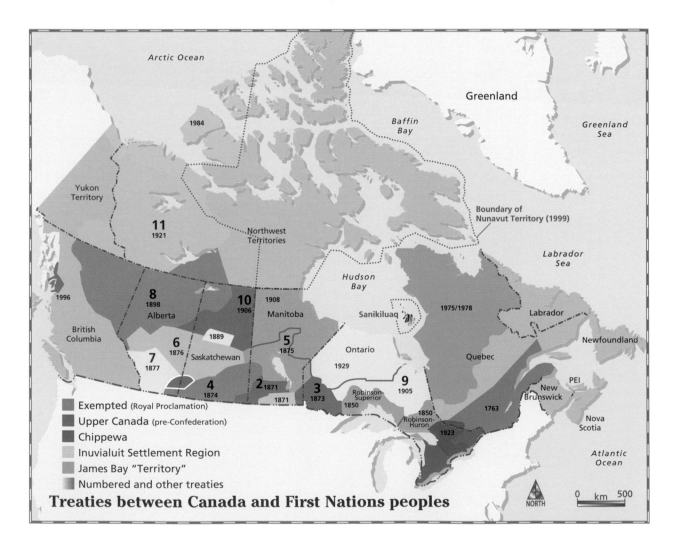

Treaties between Canada and First Nations peoples

BRITISH COLUMBIA'S FIRST MODERN-DAY TREATY

In 1996, the Nisga'a reached an agreement in principle with the governments of Canada and British Columbia that became BC's first modern-day treaty. The agreement in principle proposes a cash payment of $190 million to provide economic development and employment opportunities for the Nisga'a. It gives the Nisga'a, whose ancestors traditionally inhabited about 25 000 km^2, absolute ownership of approximately 2000 km^2 of land. The Nisga'a will assume responsibility for approximately 45 000 ha of productive forest land, an increased share of the coastal salmon fishery, and the right to control the harvest of pine mushrooms on Nisga'a lands. It also gives the Nisga'a the right to local self-government, with the responsibility to provide public services comparable to other communities in northwest British Columbia. This agreement becomes binding once it is ratified by all parties.

off between a group of Mohawks and the Canadian Army. The confrontation occurred on a reserve near Oka, Quebec, and lasted for seventy-eight days.

Settling the North-West

After Manitoba joined Confederation, many Métis moved farther west into present-day Saskatchewan and Alberta. They were looking for wide open spaces and freedom to live in the traditional Métis way. Then in the 1880s, Canadian surveyors appeared in the North-West. They started to divide that land in preparation for settlement. The railway was coming through. It would be only a matter of time before settlers would flood into their land once more. Again the Métis turned to Louis Riel for leadership. Gabriel Dumont, a respected Métis hunter and military leader, rode into the United States and persuaded Riel to return to Canada and fight for the Métis nation.

Riel Returns to the North-West

When Riel first returned to the North-West, he wanted to find a peaceful means of resolving the problem. Riel dreamed of bringing all aboriginal peoples, including the Métis, and the settlers together. The people of the North-West would speak with one voice to Ottawa about their concerns. A petition to the government was drawn up. A **petition** is a formal request to an authority for rights, privileges, or other benefits.

For the Métis, the petition demanded legal recognition that they owned the land on which they lived. They also wanted a voice in their own government. Many aboriginal peoples of the plains were struggling because of the loss of the buffalo. Their petition demanded food and money from the government in exchange for the use of their land. For the settlers, the petition protested the high price of farm machinery. They com-

Riel returns to the North-West

plained about the high costs of moving goods on the railway and demanded higher prices for their wheat. They also wanted a stronger voice for the North-West in Ottawa.

But Ottawa did not act upon the petition. By March 1885, Riel decided to wait no longer. He planned to use the same methods that had succeeded so well in Manitoba. He would set up his own government and arm his followers to pressure the Canadian government to provide a better deal for the citizens of the North-West.

It was a risky move. Conditions had changed since 1870. Now there was a police force in the North-West to support the Canadian government. There was also a railway to move troops quickly from eastern Canada.

Riel's call to take up arms lost him the support of the settlers. They wanted to see change brought about in a lawful way. Riel also lost the support of the Roman Catholic Church when he encouraged the use of arms. Only the French-speaking Métis and some other aboriginal groups continued to support him.

Among the aboriginal peoples, only chiefs Big Bear and Poundmaker and their followers joined Riel in the rebellion. These people refused to give up their way of life and move quietly onto the reserves. The early successes of Riel and the Métis gave Poundmaker and Big Bear hope. They quickly sprang into action. But what chance would Riel and his supporters have against the Canadian government?

Bloodshed in the North-West

The **North-West Rebellion** began in March 1885. A small group of North-West Mounted Police officers were defeated in a skirmish with Métis and other aboriginal peoples near Duck Lake. Ten Mounties were killed and eleven injured. The police abandoned Fort Carlton and

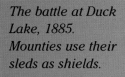
The battle at Duck Lake, 1885. Mounties use their sleds as shields.

retreated to Prince Albert. The rebellion had begun.

News of the Mountie defeat swept across the prairies. Encouraged by this Métis success, other aboriginal peoples decided to strike. One group broke into the Hudson's Bay Company store in Battleford and stole needed supplies. Big Bear's son, Wandering Spirit, led an attack on the settlement at Frog Lake. The Indian agent, two priests, and five others were killed. Other aboriginal peoples led by Chief Poundmaker headed for Battleford.

But Chief Crowfoot and most of the aboriginals of the plains refused to become involved in these battles. The federal government rushed extra supplies of flour, bacon, tea, blankets, and tobacco to them in the hope that this would keep them neutral during the conflict.

Ottawa was alarmed at the news of the Mountie defeat and decided to send troops to put down the rebellion. Within ten days, 5000 armed troops had arrived in the West. Added to this force were 500 North-West Mounted Police and fifty gov-ernment surveyors. The surveyors were especially helpful because they knew the country well.

Troops under General Middleton were to advance from Qu'Appelle to Riel's headquarters at Batoche. Another column of soldiers under Colonel Otter was to head north from Swift Current to relieve Battleford, which was surrounded by Poundmaker and his people. A third force, under General Strange, was to leave the train at Calgary and head north to track down Big Bear.

The Battles of Fish Creek and Batoche

General Middleton marched slowly towards Riel's headquarters at Batoche. He had 850 troops, a supply of cannons, and a large wagon train carrying supplies. At Fish Creek his army was ambushed in a coulee, or shallow ravine, by Gabriel Dumont and a group of Métis. Middleton lost fifty soldiers in the skirmish while four Métis were killed. It was a Métis victory and it slowed down the

The capture of Batoche by government troops

general's army two weeks. Dumont now had more time to gather a larger force of Métis and other aboriginal peoples to defend Batoche.

The Battle of Batoche

Middleton's attack on Batoche came on 9 May 1885. His plan was to use the steamboat *Northcote*, which normally carried supplies to the Hudson's Bay posts on the Saskatchewan River. He had the steamer fitted out as a gunboat. Its sides were barricaded with planks, boxes, and mattresses, behind which troops could take cover and fire on Batoche.

The *Northcote's* whistle was the signal for the attack to begin. When the whistle sounded troops would fire on Batoche from the river and General Middleton and others would attack the village on the shore. However, the first naval battle on the prairies was a disaster! Métis scouts discovered the plan and set a trap for the steamer. They stretched a steel wire across the river. As the *Northcote* approached, it struck the wire and the

smoke funnels were ripped down. The whistle came down with the smokestacks and was not able to blow the signal!

Gabriel Dumont had a plan to defend Batoche. The Métis had dug pits and trenches around the village where sharpshooters could hide and fire at approaching troops. When Middleton's troops attacked on shore, they were in full view of the Métis in their protected pits. For three days Métis defences held. But the Métis were quickly running out of ammunition. They had to resort to firing only small stones, nails, and pieces of metal. On the fourth day the Canadian troops charged the pits and the Métis were forced to surrender.

On 15 May 1885, Riel gave himself up. He wrote a letter to Middleton offering to surrender himself if the general would let the Métis go free. On the outside of the envelope, Riel scribbled the words "I do not like war." Gabriel Dumont, the old buffalo hunter, slipped through Middleton's military patrols and entered the United States.

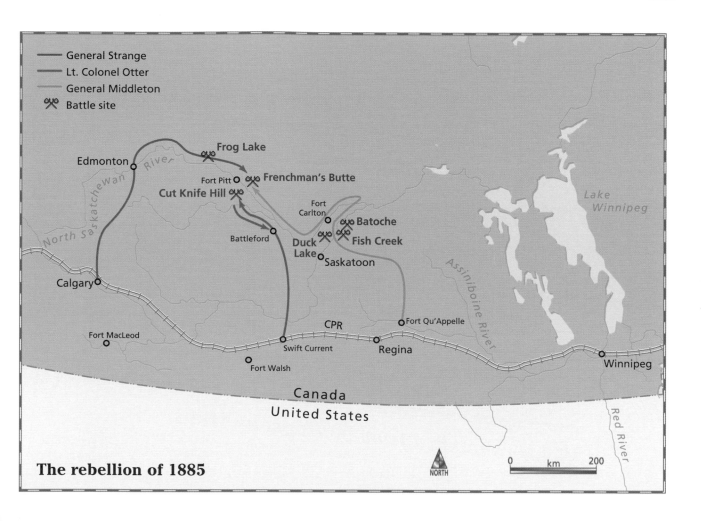

The rebellion of 1885

Legend:
- General Strange
- Lt. Colonel Otter
- General Middleton
- Battle site

Map labels: Edmonton, Frog Lake, Fort Pitt, Frenchman's Butte, Cut Knife Hill, Fort Carlton, Battleford, Batoche, Duck Lake, Fish Creek, Saskatoon, North Saskatchewan River, Calgary, Fort MacLeod, CPR, Swift Current, Fort Walsh, Fort Qu'Appelle, Regina, Winnipeg, Lake Winnipeg, Assiniboine River, Red River, Canada, United States

0 km 200 NORTH

DEVELOPING SKILLS: ANALYSING BIAS

Have you ever wondered why two historical accounts of an event can be different? How does this happen? Sometimes an event occurred so far in the past that no accurate records of it exist today. Sometimes eyewitnesses have given conflicting accounts of the event. Or sometimes the person writing about the event has brought a personal bias to it. **Bias** is a person's viewpoint or way of seeing things. A person's bias is shaped by his or her frame of reference. Personal experiences, background, family, friends, knowledge, concerns, and interests all go into the making of a person's frame of reference. Two historians writing about the North-West Rebellion may have different frames of reference. One may believe in

preserving the traditional lifestyles of the aboriginal peoples. Another may favour the idea of progress and settlement and think that the changes settlement brought were good for Canada.

Bias is not necessarily negative. Different viewpoints should invite discussion and critical thinking. But bias can be dangerous if the viewpoint is based on distorted facts or incomplete information or if it suggests that it is the only right viewpoint and excludes all others. Any point of view should carefully consider all available facts and all viewpoints. Viewpoints should always be open to change.

Frequently, French and English Canadians have looked at issues from different points of

Hamilton Gazette

Circulation 1500

May 13, 1885

Rebels stronghold destroyed!

Batoche. Eyewitness accounts reveal that General Middleton opened attack against rebel forces by cleverly fitting the steamer *Northcote* as a gunboat. A surprise attack was launched from the Saskatchewan River. Troops fired from the river at the rebels in their headquarters at Batoche. In Batoche, Métis sharpshooters huddled for protection in ground pits.

Middleton estimates rebel casualties were high. A Catholic priest reports 51 aboriginal peoples and Métis were killed at Batoche. Another 173 were wounded.

Montreal Matin

Circulation 7500

May 13, 1885

Victory snatched from courageous Métis

Batoche. Eyewitnesses claim that Middleton's attempt to attack Batoche ended in disaster. Métis scouts stretched steel wire across the Saskatchewan River, setting a trap for the steamer *Northcote*. When the so-called gunboat struck the wire, its smokestacks were torn down. The *Northcote* drifted helplessly down the river, an inglorious end to the general's battle plan.

From rifle pits dug in the ground for protection, Métis sharpshooters picked off Middleton's troops. Had they not run out of ammunition, a victory at Batoche would have been certain. Dumont reports only thirteen aboriginal peoples and Métis were killed. Only two were wounded.

view. Many people in Quebec have felt like outsiders in Canada. The province became part of the British Empire as a result of a military defeat. Their frame of reference has been formed by their background, French-Canadian culture, and their experiences in Confederation. English-Canadians also have a frame of reference shaped by their background, culture, and experiences. This frame of reference can lead to bias.

Read the two fictional accounts of the Battle of Batoche written by reporters with very different frames of reference. Then use the questions that follow to help you recognize and analyse bias.

1. a) What is the source? Who is the author? What was the author's intention?
   b) Who is the intended audience?
   c) How might these facts influence the point of view being expressed?

2. When was the material written or created? How might the time period and circumstances colour the view of events?

3. Are emotionally charged words or phrases used? What are they? Which of these present a

positive point of view? Which present a negative point of view?

4. What is fact? What is opinion? Are opinions supported by facts? (Remember that facts are information or statements that can be proven. Opinions are thoughts or feelings that may or may not be supported by facts.)

5. Does the author oversimplify? Are important facts left out?

6. Are both sides of the issue considered or is only one side presented and not the other?

7. a) Check other sources. Do they agree? If sources disagree, consider why.
   b) Which sources do you trust? Why?

8. a) What is the bias? Try to state it in one sentence.
   b) How might frame of reference account for bias?

9. How could a more balanced view be presented?

The Battle of Cut Knife Hill

In the meantime, at Battleford, frightened citizens took shelter in the North-West Mounted Police barracks. For almost a month, Battleford had lived in fear of Poundmaker and his followers. At last Colonel Otter arrived to relieve them, bringing 500 soldiers, 600 horses, and 200 wagons carrying much-needed supplies.

Colonel Otter decided to pursue Poundmaker before he and Big Bear could join forces and go on to help Riel at Batoche. Otter met Poundmaker and the Crees in a battle at Cut Knife Hill. Government troops took up position high on the hill above Poundmaker's camp. They had two cannons and an early type of machine gun, called a Gatling gun. But

Canadian troops advance on Poundmaker's camp at Cut Knife Hill

the Cree took shelter in the wooded valley below and gladly left the exposed positions to Otter's troops. Aboriginal snipers picked off Otter's troops one by one. Gradually, the aboriginal peoples encircled the base of the hill until the troops were almost completely surrounded. Otter knew that he was in serious trouble. The list of wounded soldiers was growing and soon their only line of retreat across Cut Knife Creek would be cut off. Otter gave the order to withdraw to Battleford in humiliating defeat.

Poundmaker and his followers did not follow Otter's troops. The news of Riel's defeat at Batoche convinced Poundmaker that to struggle alone was useless. Poundmaker voluntarily surrendered to General Middleton on 23 May 1885.

Farther west, General Strange and his troops met Big Bear in battle at Frenchman's Butte. The troops had the advantage of heavy guns, and Big Bear and his followers soon began to disperse. Big Bear himself avoided capture by heading north into the woods and lake country.

All through the hot days of June, the soldiers pursued Big Bear through dense bush and swamps where the mosquitoes drove troops and horses mad. By the end of June, Big Bear was out of ammunition and food, and on 2 July 1885, he surrendered to the North-West Mounted Police at Fort Carlton. The North-West Rebellion was over. From the outbreak of fighting at Duck Lake to the surrender of Big Bear, exactly 100 days had passed.

Louis Riel, Poundmaker, and Big Bear were all prisoners of the Canadian government and charged with **treason**—the crime of taking up arms against the government.

CHARACTERS IN CANADIAN HISTORY: KEY PERSONALITIES IN THE REBELLION

Poundmaker

Poundmaker was an adopted son of Crowfoot. He became a chief in 1878. How did he get his name? It seems that he had a special ability to attract buffalo into pounds. A **pound** resembled a huge corral. Sometimes a herd of buffalo were stampeded into this trap. On other occasions, the buffalo were drawn in quietly by a person like Poundmaker. He would dress in a buffalo robe and use a bell to capture the herd's curiosity. One time, it is said Poundmaker lured 500 buffalo into his pound.

Poundmaker was genuinely concerned about the welfare of his people. He did not want to see the destruction of their way of life.

Poundmaker

Gabriel Dumont

This Métis buffalo hunter was one of the most colourful figures of the North-West Rebellion of 1885. He was a crack shot. He was also an excellent rider who caught and tamed his own wild horses. After the rebellion, Dumont worked in the United States as a sharpshooter in Buffalo Bill's travelling Wild West Show.

Gabriel Dumont

Dumont and his friends plotted to rescue Riel from the Regina prison. The rescue attempt never took place. The Mounties kept Riel under constant guard using a force of 300 police officers. Not even Dumont could get his friend out of that prison!

In July 1886, the Canadian government pardoned those who had taken part in the North-West Rebellion. Dumont did not go back to the South Saskatchewan River until 1890. During the last years of his life, it is said he would sit at his cabin door and tell neighbourhood children tales of the rebellion. He would show them the scar from the wound in the head he received at Duck Lake. Then the old buffalo hunter would say, "You see, my skull was too thick for the soldiers to kill me!"

General Frederick Middleton

General Middleton

Middleton was a British general who had spent his entire career in the army. He was placed in charge of all troops sent to put down the North-West Rebellion. Why was a British general in command of Canadian troops? At this time Canada was still a colony of Britain. It was Britain's right to appoint an experienced British soldier to command the Canadian militia. The **militia** were citizens trained to defend the country and fight as an army. However, they were called into service only in times of emergency.

Middleton would have preferred to have British regular soldiers to fight in his army. He criticized the Canadian militia as "Sunday soldiers," and he did not trust the North-West Mounted Police. He was also rather stubborn and unwilling to follow advice. He did not listen to his officers, who were much more familiar with the Canadian countryside than he was. He also underestimated the fighting skills of the aboriginal peoples.

Big Bear

Big Bear

Big Bear, chief of the Plains Cree, was considered one of the most influential chiefs on the prairies. Big Bear had a stocky build and great physical strength. He was an excellent rider and buffalo hunter. While hunting or in battle, he could cling to the side of a galloping horse and shoot from the underside of the horse's neck.

Big Bear was deeply concerned about the disappearance of the buffalo, the increasing number of settlers, and the destruction of his people's way of life. He believed the treaty conditions were impossible and would leave his people in poverty. Big Bear and his followers did not want to live on reserves or accept treaty money from the government.

Earlier in his life, it is said that Big Bear had a strange dream. He saw a spring of water spouting up through the ground. He tried to stop the flow of water with his hands, but the water turned to blood and squirted through his fingers. In 1885, that dream came true. Big Bear was not able to stop the flow of blood that was shed during the North-West Rebellion.

Poundmaker presents his case to General Middleton, May 1885

Poundmaker and Big Bear on Trial

Aboriginal culture did not include the concept of **high treason**. When Poundmaker surrendered and was brought before General Middleton, he offered to shake hands. Middleton refused. The general sat on a chair with his interpreter nearby and his officers in a half circle behind him. Poundmaker and his chiefs sat on the grass before him. The general said, "Poundmaker, you are accused of high treason." However, there was no phrase for "high treason" in the Cree language. The interpreter tried to make the charge clear to Poundmaker. "You are accused of throwing sticks at the Queen and trying to knock off her bonnet" was the explanation of the charge.

Poundmaker insisted at his trial that he had not fired first at Cut Knife Hill. He also said that he was only trying to improve living conditions for his people, and pointed out that he actually saved people's lives. He held back his followers when Otter and his soldiers were retreating at Cut Knife Hill. But the jury found Poundmaker guilty. He was sentenced to three years in Stoney Mountain Penitentiary.

Big Bear was also tried for treason in Regina. He was charged with the deaths of the people at Frog Lake and with taking prisoners. Some witnesses testified that Big Bear cried out against the killings at Frog Lake. He personally protected the prisoners that his followers had captured. The chief delivered a speech in Cree to the court. He pleaded more for his people than he did for himself.

I ruled my country for long. Now I am in chains and will be sent to prison....Now I am as dead to my people. Many of them are hiding in the woods....Can this court not send them a pardon? My own children may be starving and afraid to come out of hiding. I plead to you Chiefs of the white man's laws for pity and help for the people of my band.

The country belonged to me. I may not live to see it again....I am old and ugly but I have tried to do good.... Because Big Bear has always been a friend to the white man, you should now send a pardon to my people and give them help.

But Big Bear was found guilty and sentenced to three years in the Stoney Mountain Penitentiary.

Poundmaker and Big Bear were released from prison within two years. Both returned to reservations, but died within a few months of their release.

In 1967—Canada's Centennial year—Poundmaker's bones were moved to the Cut Knife Reserve. There, a plaque was put up to honour the great chief.

In all, forty-four aboriginal people were convicted of various crimes. Eight were hanged. In addition, another eighteen Métis were eventually sent to prison for their part in the rebellion.

Riel on Trial

Riel's trial aroused great interest and excitement across Canada. Held in Regina, it has been called the most important trial in Canadian history. Six settlers, all English-speaking Protestants, were chosen as Riel's jury. But Riel was a French-speaking Roman Catholic. His friends feared he would not get a fair trial.

Riel's lawyers wanted him to plead insanity. If he were insane, he could not be held responsible for his actions. They believed it was the only way to save him. But Riel refused. For him to plead insanity would be a disgrace. It would also make his Métis followers look foolish for following an insane man.

Debate raged across the country. In Ontario, many people saw Riel as a rebel who had taken up arms against the government. They wanted him hanged! They remembered the execution of Thomas Scott. To many people in Quebec, however, Riel was a hero. He had fought to protect the rights of the French-speaking Métis nation. But Riel's jury took only one hour and twenty minutes to reach a "guilty" verdict and he was sentenced to death.

What does this cartoon suggest about Sir John A. Macdonald's position after Riel's trial?

A RIEL UGLY POSITION.

Letters from all provinces poured into Ottawa after the verdict. Sir John A. Macdonald and his Conservative government were in a difficult position. If Riel was not hanged, Ontario would be enraged and the Conservatives would lose votes there in the next election. If Riel was punished, then Quebec would be angry with the Conservative party. Macdonald, finally, decided to take his chances losing support in Quebec. "Riel shall hang," he is reported to have said, "though every dog in Quebec shall bark."

On the bright, cold day of 16 November 1885, the execution was carried out in the Regina jail. Crowds gathered quietly in English-speaking Canada to hear the news. In French-speaking Canada, however, the reaction was quite different. Flags flew at half-mast. Black-framed pictures of Riel appeared in store windows. Hundreds of students in Montreal shouted "Glory to Riel!" Likenesses of Sir John A. Macdonald were burned openly in the streets. In the newspapers and in Parliament, French-speaking Canadians blamed the death of Riel on Macdonald and English Canada. They said that he had been murdered because he was French. They asked, "Could Confederation, which had joined English and French together, manage to survive?"

Results of the 1885 Rebellion

For Aboriginal Peoples

1. The only aboriginal peoples' rebellion in Canadian history was put down by force.
2. Aboriginal peoples realized that the government was going to enforce the treaties. Since rebellion was unsuccessful, they had no other choice but to move onto the reserves.
3. Aboriginal peoples who took part in the rebellion lost their annual government payments. Their horses and ammunition were seized.

For the Métis

1. Many Métis fled to the wilderness of northern Alberta.
2. Other Métis accepted **scrip** worth $240 or 60 ha of land. They took these certificates because they remembered how they were unable to keep their land in Manitoba after 1870.
3. The proud Métis nation was broken up. Not until the twentieth century were Métis organizations formed again to improve conditions for their people.

For French-English Relations

1. The split between English-speaking and French-speaking people over the Riel affair was bitter in Canada. Neither side forgave the other for its view of Riel.
2. Hard feelings between the Ontario Protestants and the Quebec Catholics lasted a long time after Riel's execution.

For Political Parties

1. Many people in Quebec stopped voting for the Conservative party because it had hanged Riel.
2. Many people in Quebec began to vote for the Liberal party. This was especially true after the Liberals chose a French-Canadian leader, Wilfrid Laurier.

For Western Canada

1. The CPR was completed to carry troops to the West.
2. Settlers felt more secure moving to the West because the rebellions had been put down.
3. Many soldiers who fought in the rebellion settled in the West.

ACTIVITIES

Check Your Understanding

1. Add these new words to your *Factfile*.

   • Cypress Hills Massacre • Fort Whoop-Up • North-West Mounted Police • treaty
   • agents • annuity • aboriginal rights • reserve • Battle of Duck Lake • Battle of
   Fish Creek • high treason • Battle of Batoche • plea of insanity • Battle of Cut
   Knife Hill

2. a) What were the two main tasks that the North-West Mounted Police had been
      sent out West to do?
   b) Why were these tasks necessary in the 1870s?

3. Study the map on page 130.
   a) Examine the location of the areas covered by each of the numbered treaties.
      Identify the parts of the present-day provinces surrendered by each treaty.
   b) What parts of the West were not covered by treaties?
   c) Examine the dates when the treaties were signed. What does this suggest to you
      about how the West was opened?

4. In what ways did the signing of the treaties mean the end of a way of life for the
   aboriginal peoples of the plains?

5. a) On an outline map of western Canada, locate the following places. Use an atlas
      to help you.

North Saskatchewan River	South Saskatchewan River
CPR	Duck Lake
Batoche	Winnipeg
Battleford	Fort Carlton
Swift Current	Regina
Cut Knife	Prince Albert

   b) Devise symbols to mark each battle site in the North-West Rebellion and indi-
      cate who was fighting whom at each location.

6. a) Why would Riel be considered a hero in Quebec?
   b) How did the Riel situation create problems for Sir John A. Macdonald?
   c) How did the people of Ontario react to Quebec's opinion of Riel? Why?

Confirm Your Learning

7. Read "A Cree Legend" below and answer the questions that follow.

A Cree Legend

*Long ago a Whiteman came from across the sea to our land. He spoke to our
ancestor, who was sitting on a huge log.*

"Move over," said the Whiteman.

Our ancestor moved over a little and the Whiteman sat on the log. The Whiteman nudged him and again said, "Move over." The Indian moved over a little.

Soon the Whiteman repeated, "Move over."

This happened again and again until our ancestor was pushed off the log. Then the Whiteman said, "The log is now mine."

Our ancestor took off his hat and respectfully asked, "May I sit on one part of the log?"

"No," said the Whiteman, "I am using all of the log. But the stump of the tree is nearby. Why don't you sit on it?"

Since then the Indians have been sitting on the very small stump and hoping that the Whiteman would never want it.

Recounted at Shamattawa, Manitoba.

a) Why is the aboriginal person sitting alone on the log at the beginning of the legend? What does the log represent?

b) What happened when the first Europeans arrived in the country?

c) What happened as more and more settlers arrived in the country?

d) What evidence is there in the legend that the aboriginal peoples welcomed the Europeans and showed friendliness towards them?

e) Tell the legend in your own words and give it a title.

8. In western Canada, aboriginal groups were settled onto reserves without the bloodshed that occurred in the United States. Some people say that this was largely due to the help and presence of the North-West Mounted Police. Explain why.

9. Why would the First Nations see the treaties as "broken promises"?

10. Role-play a council meeting of aboriginal chiefs who are trying to decide whether or not to join Riel in his fight. Include Big Bear, Poundmaker, and Crowfoot. Be sure you consider the following:

a) the role of the North-West Mounted Police

b) the soldiers' military strength

c) feelings among aboriginal peoples

d) problems facing aboriginal peoples.

11. Review the steps for interpreting political cartoons in Chapter 2 on pages 51–52. Practise your skills by interpreting the political cartoon "A Riel Ugly Position" on page 141.

Challenge Your Mind

12. Discuss: "The Mounted Police made the Canadian West a different kind of place than the American West."

13. Debate: "The numbered treaties were unfair to aboriginal peoples."

14. How do you think the Blackfoot felt when they found out the treaties took away the land for all time? Imagine you are a descendant of a Blackfoot who signed this treaty. How would you feel about the treaty your ancestor signed? Why? Why do some descendants of aboriginal peoples who signed the treaties refer to these deals as "broken promises"?

15. Crowfoot consulted with many of his people about signing Treaty No 7. One of these was an old man named Pemmican. Pemmican was known for his great wisdom. His advice was often sought by the Blackfoot. When Crowfoot asked if they should sign the treaty, this is what Pemmican answered:

…Your life henceforth will be different from what it has been. Buffalo makes your body strong. What you will eat from this money will have your people buried all over these hills. You will be tied down, you will not wander the plains; the settlers will take your land and fill it. You won't have your own free will; they will lead you by a halter. That is why I say don't sign.

Pemmican's words turned out to be prophetic.
a) What does "prophetic" mean?
b) In what ways did Pemmican's words come true?

16. What steps do you think the government would have taken if aboriginal peoples had not agreed to sign the treaties?

17. Collect newspaper and magazine clippings on aboriginal rights and First Nations land claims today. As a group project, make a large scrapbook of your clippings. Write letters to the editors of local newspapers expressing your opinions about aboriginal land claims.

18. Do you think that the Métis should have fought against the government? Can you think of anything they could have done instead?

19. Divide your class into groups and put Riel on trial. You will need a judge, a prosecuting lawyer, a defending lawyer, Riel, a six-person jury, witnesses, reporters, and spectators. If you decide not to hang Riel, what else can you do with him? Did Riel get a fair trial in your class? In Regina in 1885? Explain your answer.

20. One of the members of the jury at Louis Riel's trial later said: "We tried Riel for treason and hanged him for the murder of Scott." What do you think the juror meant? Was it a fair summary of what happened? Why or why not?

Chief Crowfoot with his family. The Blackfoot were one aboriginal nation directly affected by western settlement. They signed Treaty No. 7 in 1877. At the signing, Crowfoot said, "We cannot sell the lives of men and animals, and therefore we cannot sell the land. It was put here by the Great Spirit...."

CHAPTER 6

Settling the West

HOMESTEADING ON THE PRAIRIES

That April of 1883 was still bitterly cold when the Willoughby family unloaded all their possessions from the colonist train at Moose Jaw. They came west early in the spring so there would be time to get a crop planted that year.

Next day at dawn, the wagons were loaded and they set out on the trail to find their new homestead. They had to move slowly because the horses, which they had brought with them, were not used to western trails. A few of the settlers had oxen. Though slower, the oxen were stronger. Oxen could also be used to pull a plough to break through the tough prairie sod. If all else failed, oxen could be eaten.

After a few days on the trail, a terrible spring blizzard struck. The travellers were trapped in tents for three days. Some of their horses died during the storm. A few of the settlers gave up then and there and headed back to Moose Jaw.

The others struggled on. They left some of their possessions on the prairie to lighten the loads for the surviving horses. The prairie winds cut their faces like razors. Wagons had to be floated across

American settler John Ware and family around 1896. The Wares moved to the Canadian West in 1882 and established a successful ranch .

icy rivers and streams. As the weather cleared, spring mud buried wagon wheels to their axles. Sometimes the wagons had to be unloaded, pushed out of the mud, and then reloaded.

Only a few kilometres could be covered each day. Every night there were the added tasks of setting up camp, gathering fuel, and cooking meals. But finally the journey ended. Guided by rough maps, the settlers began to search in brush and prairie grass for the surveyors' stakes. When they found them, they could unload their wagons for the last time. The homesteaders were home.

But home was really just a spot on the prairies. A house still had to be built and the ground broken. No sign of another human life could be seen. To the new homesteader, there was the feeling of being completely alone in a new land.

The ranch established by the Ware family

Surveying the Land

As early as the summer of 1869, the government had sent surveyors to the West. They were there to measure and map the vast western lands so they could be divided into farms for settlers. All the land west of Fort Garry to the Rocky Mountains was to be surveyed.

There were three steps in the division of the land:

1. The land was divided into townships.

Each **township** was a square with sides almost 10 km in length.

2. Each township was subdivided into 36 sections. A **section** was a perfect square with each side measuring 1.6 km. Sections were numbered 1 through 36, starting in the southeast corner. Section 8 and part of section 26 were kept by the Hudson's Bay Company. The other even-numbered sections belonged to the Canadian government. These were free home-

stead lands for settlers. Sections 11 and 29 were school lands. The other odd-numbered sections were set aside as railway lands. The CPR could sell these sections to raise money for the construction of the railway.

Free homestead lands	31	32	33	34	35	36
School lands	30	29	28	27	26	25
Hudson's Bay Co. lands	19	20	21	22	23	24
Railway lands	18	17	16	15	14	13
	7	8	9	10	11	12
	1	2	3	4	5	6

A prairie township

3. Each section was then divided into quarters. A **quarter section** contained 65 ha. Each quarter was marked out by direction, like this:

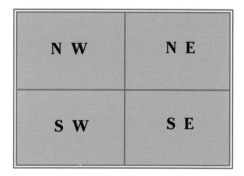

N W	N E
S W	S E

The Dominion Land Act, 1872

The **Dominion Land Act**, also called the Homestead Act, was enacted in 1872. Any adult or head of a family could claim a quarter section from the land set aside for homesteads. All they had to pay was a

$10 registration fee. They were required to live on the land for six months each year, build a house, and start to cultivate the land. If the settlers carried out these conditions in three years, full ownership was turned over to them. Homesteaders could then buy more land for about $5 a hectare.

The Sod House Frontier

The first task facing homesteaders was to build a shelter. Over much of the prairies there were no large trees, so the settlers used the only material available—prairie sod. The **sod house** and the sod barn became the mark of the prairie frontier.

The greatest advantage of sod buildings was that they were cheap. A family reported that the total cash cost of their sod house was $2.97. That was for one window, a roof jack, door hinges, and a door latch.

To construct a sod house, trenches were ploughed for the bottom of the walls. Then sod, thick with plenty of roots, was chosen from a dry, grassy creek bed. The pieces of sod were cut into strips and hauled to the building site on wagons. They were placed grass-side down and piled like bricks, but no mortar was used. If it was possible to find light poplar poles, they were placed on the tops of the walls to form a roof. Hay was spread on the poles, and sod placed on top. Most sod houses had a dirt floor and a dirt roof.

If it rained, the roof of a sod house became so full of water that it dripped for days. A woman who was born on a rainy day in a sod shack with a dirt roof told this story. The roof was leaking so badly that they had to hold an umbrella over her mother while she was being born. Another disadvantage was that mice and insects sometimes came with the sod!

Thousands of these sod houses were built all across the prairies. The thick walls kept the buildings warm in winter and cool in summer. Even in the middle of winter, water in a kettle would not freeze in a sod house if the fire went out at night. There were few windows in a sod building because the holes would weaken the walls.

Another advantage of a sod house was that it was almost completely fireproof. Dreaded prairie fires just could not burn down a sod house.

Neighbours would gather around to help newcomers put up a sod house and barn. This was called a **sodding bee**, and a house could be built in a day. Neighbours provided food for the workers, and at night, a fiddle might be brought out and an open-air dance held to welcome the new family into the community.

A sod house on the prairie. Can you describe how it was built?

CHARACTERS IN CANADIAN HISTORY: INVENTORS

Jane and David Fife

If the Fife's cow had taken one more bite, Canada might never have become a great wheat-producing country. It happened like this. Jane and David Fife came from Scotland in 1820 and settled near Peterborough, Ontario. David Fife spent a lot of time experimenting with wheat. He was trying to develop a strong and healthy kind of wheat that would grow well in Canada. Although his neighbours laughed at him, he continued to mix different strains.

Jane and David Fife

Marquis wheat

In 1843, Fife sowed a few wheat seeds that he had received in the mail from a friend in Glasgow. The seeds had originally come from Europe. Fife planted the seeds behind his house. Only one plant had healthy stalks with good fat heads. Fife decided to save the seeds from that plant.

Shortly before the wheat was ripe, the Fife's cow broke into the garden. Jane Fife looked out the window just as the cow was about to munch the heads of the experimental wheat. She ran from the house waving her apron and shooing the cow out of the yard. The precious wheat had been saved.

From the seeds of that one plant came a new type of wheat known as Red Fife. It was a hardy strain that could resist common wheat diseases. Most significant was that it matured ten days earlier than other kinds of wheat. This was important on the prairies, where the frost-free growing season is short. Soon many prairie farmers were growing and harvesting Red Fife.

Charles Saunders

Charles Saunders was a quiet, studious man in charge of the government's experimental farm in Ottawa. At the turn of the twentieth century, Saunders took Red Fife wheat and crossed it with a variety from India. It grew into a healthy strain that Saunders called Marquis. Marquis wheat was the discovery of the century. It was even better for the Canadian growing season because it took just 100 days to ripen. Now even the northern prairies could be opened for farming. With the development of Marquis wheat, Canada was to become one of the greatest wheat-producing nations in the world.

Abraham Gesner

Abraham Gesner was a Nova Scotia doctor, geologist, author, and inventor. In 1842 in New Brunswick, he opened one of the first museums in British North America. It featured a collection of minerals and wildlife specimens that he had collected on his travels through the countryside.

Gesner's greatest accomplishment, however, came in 1854. He patented the process for manufacturing kerosene oil from petroleum. Kerosene was inexpensive to manufacture. It burned with a light that was both brilliant and white. In fact, when the first kerosene lamp was lit in a home at the Red River Settlement, it

Abraham Gesner

gave off such a glow that the neighbours ran to help put out the flames. They thought the house was on fire. Soon kerosene lamps replaced candles and whale oil lamps. The light from a kerosene lamp was much easier to read and work by. Gesner's invention made him an important forerunner of today's giant petrochemical industry.

The Icelanders

One of the first groups to take up homesteads were Icelanders. Four hundred people docked at Quebec in 1874 on their way to homes in the United States. They were fleeing volcanic eruptions in their home country. The government invited them to stay in Canada, promising them freedom and Canadian citizenship, a large tract of land where they could farm and fish, and their own language and customs.

Sigtryggur Jonasson, their leader, selected a place on the west shore of Lake Winnipeg to settle. They named the place Gimli, or paradise, after the home of the Norse gods. An Icelandic community exists there today, and Jonasson is still remembered as the founder of Icelandic settlement in Canada.

The first winter for the Icelanders was anything but paradise. The settlers didn't arrive at Gimli until late summer and had no time to build houses before an early winter set in. They were forced to live in buffalo tents belonging to the Hudson's Bay Company. In one of them, the first Icelandic Canadian was born. There were many deaths from starvation and scurvy that winter. The fishing nets they brought from Iceland had mesh that was too large to catch lake fish, and wild game was scarce. The following year, in 1876, a smallpox epidemic struck the colony and many people died. Those who were left burned down their cabins to destroy the germs.

The first group of Icelandic immigrants

Fortunately, the little colony survived. The Icelanders went on to develop the inland fishing industry in the lakes and rivers of Manitoba. They caught Winnipeg goldeye and sturgeon and sent them to markets in Winnipeg and eastern Canada.

In the midst of these trying conditions, many settlers taught their children to read and write. Jon Gudmundson regularly published a small newspaper that first winter. He wrote it in his own handwriting and read it aloud to groups as he travelled from house to house. Today, Winnipeg has one of the largest Icelandic populations of any city outside Iceland.

CHARACTERS IN CANADIAN HISTORY: MARGRET BENEDICTSSON

Many Icelandic women made special contributions to the history of Canada. One was Margret Benedictsson. In the early 1900s, she and some women in the Icelandic community campaigned with other women in Manitoba for the right to vote. By January 1916, their efforts met with success. Manitoba was the first province in Canada to grant women the vote.

The petition by the Political Equality League for the enfranchisement of women in Manitoba

The Mennonites

Mennonite settlers came from Russia to find religious freedom. Their faith demanded that they should never go to war. In 1874, they left their homeland when the Russian government ordered them to serve in the army.

Between 1874 and 1876, the Mennonites settled west of the Red River. They were already experienced in farming the rich prairies of Russia and knew that the prairie soil would be good for growing grain. In 1876, one observer wrote:

Seldom have I beheld any spectacle more full of promise of a successful future than the Mennonite settlement. When I

A Mennonite family farm. How would you describe this farm?

visited these people, they had only been in the province two years. Yet, in a long ride I took across many miles of prairies, which but yesterday were absolutely bare....I passed village after village, homestead after homestead, furnished with all the conveniences of European comfort and up-to-date farming methods. On either side of the road cornfields were already ripe for harvest, and pastures were full of herds of cattle.

From *Extraordinary Tales from Manitoba History*, by J.W. Chafe.

Thus, the Mennonites were the first to prove the open prairie could be farmed successfully.

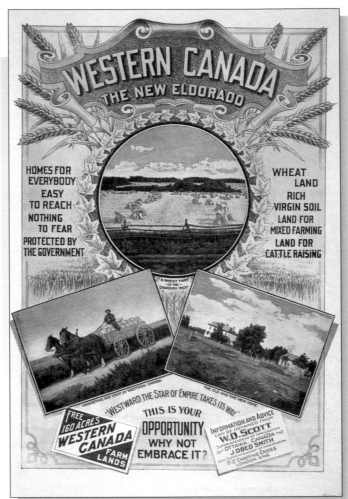

A poster advertising Canada's West to settlers. What impressions does it give?

A Slow Start to Immigration

Though the Dominion Land Act had provided free homesteads since 1872, large numbers of settlers did not come to Canada in these early years. From 1881 to 1896, settlers took up only 56 000 homesteads in the west, and abandoned 16 000 of these. In 1896, only 16 835 immigrants came to Canada, the lowest number since 1868. In fact, during the previous fifteen years, the number of Canadians going to the United States was greater than the number of immigrants coming to Canada. Suddenly, however, things changed. A new prime minister, Wilfrid Laurier, and a new minister of the interior from the West, Clifford Sifton, took office in 1896. The Canadian Pacific Railway joined the government in the country's biggest advertising campaign—to sell "the Golden North-West" to people in Britain, the United States, Europe, and eastern Canada.

Sifton and his agents set out to persuade people from other parts of the world to come and settle the prairies. The government was looking for strong, healthy settlers experienced in farming. They would have to break up the soil, put up farm buildings, and survive the Canadian winters.

The government ran advertising campaigns describing the opportunities available in western Canada. Eventually, the advertising paid off. Sifton's policies launched a flood of immigration to the Canadian West.

Other factors also helped to make Canada's immigration plan work, however. There was not much good farmland left in the United States, so settlers were attracted by the good free land available in Canada. In Europe, the demand for Canadian wheat almost doubled, which made wheat farming more profitable for Canadian farmers. Canada's transcontinental railway could now ship grain to markets, and steam-powered ocean vessels could transport wheat to Europe cheaply and quickly. The invention of modern farm machinery, such as ploughs and reapers, helped make farmers' work easier and more efficient. Finally, millions of Europeans were looking for better opportunities. Some were fleeing economic hardships, political repression, compulsory military service, and overcrowded conditions. Many chose Canada.

Sifton's policy, however, was selective. He admired the peasant farmers of Europe. They were hard-working, experienced farmers with large families to work the land. He also favoured American farmers known as "dry-landers." They knew how to grow crops on western lands that had very little rain. Sifton restricted the entry of Asians, Blacks, Jews, East Indians, and southern Europeans. People from these cultures came to Canada later when the country's immigration policy became more open. Still, Sifton's immigration drive resulted in enormous population growth.

A Dutch poster inviting new immigrants to Canada. Can you translate the message?

Ukrainian families on board a ship to Canada. What might they be expecting upon their arrival?

DEVELOPING SKILLS: INTERPRETING DATA IN TABLES

You have probably come across tables of data in magazines, newspapers, and textbooks. Tables are just a short-form means of communicating information. It would probably take several paragraphs to describe in sentences all the information you can present in a simple table. The secret to using tables effectively is to recognize their main features and understand how they present information.

Helpful Hints

1. Read the title. The title tells you the main purpose of the table. Why was it prepared? What is it about? What are the limits of its contents?
2. Note the units. What are the actual units that the numbers represent? The units are usually given in the title, in the columns or rows, or in the footnotes.
3. Scan the format. Tables are set up in columns, which present information vertically (up and down), and rows, which present information across the page. In Table 1 on page 157, for example, the first column tells the year. The top row shows the immigrants to Canada from Britain, the United States, and other countries and the total from 1897 to 1905.
4. Interpret the data. To determine any changes, increases, or decreases from the data in the

table, you have to make comparisons. Table 1 on page 157 is organized chronologically from 1897 to 1905. To see a pattern or trend in immigration from each of these areas, you would have to read down the columns. But if you want to see which part of the world provided the most immigrants to Canada, you have to read across the top row. If you want to know which area provided the most immigrants at any time covered by the table, you have to use information from both columns and rows.

5. Note the source of the data. Knowing who compiled the data helps you to assess the accuracy of the information. Is it a reliable and unbiased source? The Dominion Bureau of Statistics is considered accurate and reliable.

Try It!

Examine the information in Table 1. What conclusions can you draw from the data? Use the following questions as a guide.

1. What is the purpose of the table and the years covered?
2. Did the total number of immigrants increase every year from 1897 to 1905?
3. a) What does Column 3 tell you?

American settlers from Colorado arrive in the Canadian West, 1914

b) What does Row 2 tell you?

c) What does the figure in Column 3, Row 4 tell you?

4. a) What general trend or pattern over time do the data reveal about immigration to Canada from Britain?

b) What is the general trend in immigration from the United States over the same period?

c) What is the general trend in Canadian immigration from other countries over the same period?

5. Which area of the world provided the most immigrants to Canada in 1897, 1900, 1903, and 1905?

6. Which year saw the greatest number of immigrants coming to Canada? the smallest number of immigrants coming to Canada?

7. According to the data, was Clifford Sifton's plan a success? What are the reasons for your opinion?

8. Examine Table 2. State two conclusions you can draw from this table.

Table 1: Number of Immigrants to Canada, 1897–1905

	From Britain	From the United States	From other countries	Total
1897	11 383	2 412	7 921	21 716
1898	11 173	9 119	11 608	31 900
1899	10 660	11 945	21 938	44 543
1900	10 282	17 086	20 422	47 790
1901	11 810	17 987	19 352	49 149
1902	17 259	26 388	23 732	67 379
1903	41 792	49 473	37 099	128 364
1904	50 374	45 171	34 786	130 331
1905	65 359	43 543	37 364	146 266

Dominion Bureau of Statistics.

Table 2: Population of the Prairie Provinces

Year	Manitoba	Saskatchewan	Alberta	Total
1871	25 288	Saskatchewan and Alberta		73 228
1891	152 506	Saskatchewan and Alberta		251 473
1901	255 211	91 279	73 022	419 512
1911	461 394	492 432	374 295	1 328 121
1921	610 118	757 510	588 454	1 956 082

Canada: Unity in Diversity, Cornell, Hamelin, Ouellet, and Trudel, Holt, Rinehart, and Winston

The Importance of Railways to the Prairie Building Boom

The railway made it possible for western settlements to grow quickly. The steam engine was as important to opening up the prairies as the canoe had been to the development of the fur trade. Trains hauled passengers, goods, and mail across the plains and over the mountain passes. They also carried wheat and timber back to distant customers.

The early years of the twentieth century saw intense activity in railway building. In 1903, the Canadian Northern began constructing a line to link eastern Saskatchewan to Edmonton, along with a branch line extending 160 km north from Prince Albert. At the same time the Grand Trunk Pacific started to build a line linking Winnipeg to Prince Rupert through the Yellowhead Pass. Because of the prosperity, the Canadian Pacific Railway was also expanding. Branch lines across the southern prairies brought rail service closer to the settlers. It was estimated that a farmer living more than 16 km from a railway faced difficult transportation problems. The whole agricultural system depended on the railway to move machinery and livestock into the community and agricultural products out.

Towns were needed to service farming communities. Prairie towns and villages grew up around railway stations and grain elevators where the wheat crop was weighed and stored until boxcars arrived to haul it all away. In each region a large city emerged because of the railway. Winnipeg, located where the Red and Assiniboine rivers meet, emerged as the port of entry to the West. It was there that the offices of the grain elevator companies, railway communications, and telegraph and telephone companies were

A grain elevator on the prairies

The railway brought settlers and goods to the West

First Nations Land Issues in British Columbia

concentrated. By 1911, Winnipeg was the largest city in western Canada.

Regina, Saskatoon, Edmonton, and Calgary were once small, isolated outposts. Now they also became large thriving trading and railway centres. For example, between 1901 and 1906, the population of Edmonton grew from 2630 to 11 170.

The Importance of Railways in the Growth of British Columbia

In British Columbia, the Canadian Pacific Railway was the main route across the province. Branch lines to the United States helped to transport mineral and agricultural products to markets. The building of the Grand Trunk's western terminus at Prince Rupert made it possible to open up a number of northern valleys of British Columbia to settlement and development. The building of the Canadian Northern opened up new areas along the North Thompson River. The Peace River country was not linked by rail to Vancouver until after the Second World War. The West was booming and the population of Canada was growing.

The advance of farmers, miners, ranchers, and loggers into developing areas of the province angered the aboriginal peoples whose lands were being taken over. The ownership of land was always the major issue. Aboriginal peoples sent letters and petitions to governments demanding recognition of aboriginal title and asking for treaties. In 1906, a Squamish and Nisga'a delegation of three travelled to London, England, to appeal to King Edward VII. The aboriginal leaders were told that land questions were purely a matter for the Canadian government.

The years from 1916 to 1927 were fateful for aboriginal land questions and political activity. In 1916, the Allied Indian Tribes was formed, representing the majority of aboriginal groups. The Allied Indian Tribes was opposed to the recommendations of the McKenna-McBride Commission, which had been set up to investigate the issue of Indian reserves in the province of British Columbia. In spite of First Nations opposition and without their consent, the federal government passed the BC Indian Lands Settlement Act. This act resulted in reserve land being set at only 0.36 per cent of the total area of British Columbia. The government took further action to curb mounting aboriginal protest. In 1927, aboriginal peoples were prohibited from raising money or retaining lawyers to pursue land claims. This law made it impossible for the Allied Indian Tribes to exist because pursuing land claims was one of its major objectives.

DEVELOPING SKILLS: WRITING A RESEARCH ESSAY

"We live in an information age. "You've heard this said many times, and it is quite true. Our success in and out of school often depends on how well we can find information to answer questions, and how well we can present our point of view. In any occupation or career, you will be called upon to process information, make decisions, and present your ideas clearly. Planning and writing a research essay is excellent practice for the job and life skills you will need for the future.

Earlier, you may have done a research report on a topic related to the gold rush. A report, however, is different from an essay. In a report, you present facts to describe or explain. In an essay, you present facts to support a particular point of view or argument. Writing an essay can be fun because it gives you a chance to argue and persuade other people that your ideas have merit.

■ Step 1: Thesis

Every essay needs a thesis. A **thesis** tells what you are going to prove in an essay. It clearly states your argument.

How do you formulate a thesis? Suppose your topic is Clifford Sifton's campaign to fill the West with settlers. First, do your research. Use books, magazines, films, and computer databases to investigate your topic. Decide on two or three main subtopics for your research. For example, you need to know what problems Sifton faced, what strategies he used to solve these problems, and how successful his campaign was.

Next, review all the information you have collected and let it ferment in your brain. As ideas are twisting and turning through your head, you will be formulating a point of view. For example, you may have found out that Sifton's plan was to keep the name of Canada constantly in front of the people of Britain, the United States, and eastern Europe. This is the basis for your thesis.

■ Step 2: Thesis Statement

State your thesis clearly in a sentence. For example: *Sifton's plan for settling the West was to keep the name of Canada constantly in front of potential settlers from Britain, the United States, and eastern Europe.* This thesis statement clearly summarizes your point of view or argument.

■ Step 3: Essay Outline

Prepare an outline for your essay like the one below. Use this outline to organize your ideas and the facts gathered in your research. Each paragraph should state a main idea to help prove your thesis (argument), and include subpoints (facts) to support the main idea. For example, the main point in paragraph 2 may be that it was impossible for a British citizen to miss all the signs and posters advertising the "Garden West" and inviting them to move to Canada. Your subpoints should give specific examples and evidence to support this idea.

Outline	
Paragraph 1	Introduce Thesis
Paragraph 2	Main Point
	•Subpoint
	•Subpoint
	•Subpoint
Paragraph 3	Main Point
	•Subpoint
	•Subpoint
	•Supoint
Paragraph 4	Main Point
	•Sub-point
	•Subpoint
	•Subpoint
Paragraph 5	Summarize and Restate Thesis

■ Step 4: Write Your Essay

Once you have organized your ideas in an outline, you are ready to write your essay. Concentrate on presenting your ideas clearly and persuasively. Make sure that your facts clearly support your thesis.

■ Step 5: Sum Up Your Arguments

In your concluding paragraph, sum up all your main arguments. Be sure you show how your arguments prove the thesis you stated in your introductory paragraph. As a final point, build on your thesis by restating it in different words.

■ Step 6: Review Your Essay

Try to allow time to set your essay aside for a few days or a week. Then reread it. You will have a fresh perspective on your work.

Ask yourself the following questions:

- Is my thesis statement clear?
- Do my arguments in each paragraph clearly support my thesis?
- Do the facts I have presented clearly support each argument?
- Is my essay persuasive?

- Can I make it better? Do I need to make any revisions?
- Is it grammatically correct?

Try It!

Write a mini research essay on one of the following topics, or on a topic of your choice:

- Clifford Sifton's plan to settle the West
- The effect of immigration on aboriginal peoples
- The selective nature of Sifton's immigration policy
- The importance of the European peasant farmers to the settlement of the prairies
- The early Icelandic community in western Canada
- How the railway influenced immigration
- The influence of the railway on western settlement patterns

Gold in the Klondike

During the summer of 1896, George Carmack, Skookum Jim, and Tagish Charlie staked a claim along Rabbit Creek in the Klondike. There in the Yukon they found gold lying in cracks of rock "thick between the flaky slabs of rock like cheese sandwiches." Carmack called his discovery Bonanza Creek.

When word got out, thousands of men, and some women, from the United States, Europe, Canada, and as far away as Australia headed for Bonanza Creek.

Most sailed to Skagway, Alaska, and struggled over the **Trail of '98**. They had to climb 1000 m through the Chilkoot Pass to the headwaters of the Yukon River. In the winter of 1897, 22 000 people were checked through the Chilkoot Pass by the North-West Mounted Police. Each person was required by the police to carry in a year's supply of food, tents, equipment, and clothing. The goods weighed about a tonne in all. Miners had to go up and down that steep slope of snow and ice many times until all their supplies were across. In one year, only 2000 out of 10 000 miners who set out from Skagway completed the trip. Many died along the way, while others turned back. If they made it across the pass, they built rafts and boats and floated 800 km downstream to the goldfields.

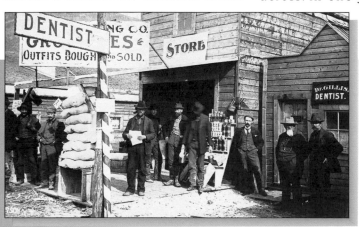

Gold Rush in the Klondike

A PROSPECTOR'S PROVISIONS

It was suggested that each prospector should take the following provisions to the goldfields:

180 kg flour	5 kg tea	pepper
45 kg beans	14 kg coffee	cooking
45 kg bacon	70 kg mixed fruit	utensils
45 kg sugar	salt	

In addition, each person should be outfitted with the following:

3 suits heavy woollen underwear	1 leather fur-lined coat	1 pair hip rubber boots	1 pair woollen mitts
4 pairs heavy stockings	1 pair jeans lined with flannel	1 pair heavy miner's boots	1 sleeping bag
2 pairs heavy socks	1 Mackinaw coat	1 pair heavy overshoes	1 sleeping cap
1 pair hunting stockings	1 pair Mackinaw trousers	4 blankets	4 canvas carrying bags
1 heavy sweater	1 suit buckskin underwear	1 pair leather-lined mitts	tools, including: 2 miner's pans, picks, shovels, axes, saw, file, and knife
1 lighter sweater			

Dawson City was born at the spot where the Klondike flows into the Yukon River. Within two years it had become the largest Canadian city west of Winnipeg. Dawson City's music halls, hotels, saloons, stores, shacks, and tents became the centre of the Gold Rush. More than forty restaurants and twelve hotels provided food, entertainment, and meeting places for the prospectors. In its stores people could be outfitted with miner's gear or the latest fashions from Paris! But prices were high. A sack of flour in 1897 cost $75.00, and eggs were $18.00 a dozen! There were two daily newspapers to report the latest news of those who struck it rich.

The Yukon was a rough and wild place during the Gold Rush, but thanks to the Mounties, it was not lawless. Superintend-

ent Sam Steele and about 200 Mounties ruled with an iron hand. They handled situations not by brute force, but by common sense, tact, and fearlessness. As a result, the Yukon did not experience the serious crime that existed in many other gold rush areas of the world.

Frontier justice was swift and severe for any prospector who broke the rules. Rather than go to the trouble of hunting daily, some miners robbed the **caches** of the aboriginal peoples. Such actions

Mounties in the Yukon during the Gold Rush

threatened to upset the good relations most prospectors enjoyed with aboriginal peoples. As a result, miners became their own lawmakers and enforcers. They issued harsh punishment to those who stole food and usually banished them from the Klondike.

In the best year, 1900, $22 million worth of gold was taken from the Klondike. Although some miners did get rich, most spent all the gold they found. Many left the Klondike poorer than they were when they arrived! But in seven years, nearly $100 million in gold had been extracted from the area. By 1903, the boom was over. Mining in the Yukon declined. But in southern British Columbia, more stable mining enterprises were started when copper, lead, zinc, and silver were found.

THE SPELL OF THE YUKON

I wanted the gold, and I sought it;
  I scrabbled and mucked like a slave.
Was it famine or scurvy—I fought it;
  I hurled my youth into a grave.
I wanted the gold, and I got it—
  Came out with a fortune last fall,—
Yet somehow life's not what I thought it,
  And somehow the gold isn't all....
There's gold, and it's haunting and haunting;
  It's luring me on as of old;
Yet it isn't the gold that I'm wanting
  So much as just finding the gold.
It's the great, big, broad land 'way up yonder,
  It's the forests where silence has lease;
It's the beauty that thrills me with wonder,
  It's the stillness that fills me with peace.

                    Robert Service

The Collected Poems of Robert Service. Toronto: McGraw-Hill, 1963.

A 'grizzly' for washing gold

Two New Provinces and Two New Territories

The astonishing population growth of the North-West soon brought demands for changes in the way the people were governed. In 1888, the federal government had granted the North-West a legislated assembly. The Lieutenant-Governor could take the advice of the Assembly if he wished, but he sometimes ignored the Assembly. And he still controlled how money would be spent. In other words, the North-West did not yet have responsible government. It was in exactly the same position that Upper and Lower Canada were in during the 1830s.

Frederick W. Haultain was a leader in the North-West who argued for more responsible government. Gradually, the powers of the North-West Territories Assembly were increased by the federal government. By 1892, the Assembly's power had been increased, and the Assembly had won the right to say how federal subsidies of money should be spent.

Haultain also supported the idea of provincial status for the territories. He wanted the creation of one province, while other prominent westerners, such as R.B. Bennett, argued for two. Laurier delayed creating new provinces because he believed that there were not enough people in the territories.

By 1905, the growing population in the territories was demanding action. In this year, two new provinces were created— Alberta and Saskatchewan. According to the act that created these provinces, the federal government decided on three important issues for the new provinces. The federal government retained ownership of public lands in each province. The provinces would receive more than $1 million, and each year would receive federal subsidies for public works. Taxes in the new provinces could be used to set up Protestant or Catholic schools.

The new western provinces differed from the old eastern provinces. Few people had been born in the West, but had come there from other parts of Canada, and from the United States, Britain, and Europe. There were many languages, nationalities, and religions. The population was widely scattered, and men greatly outnumbered women. In 1916, the population was young. The average age was less than twenty-five years.

Celebrations in Edmonton as Alberta joins Confederation

Seventy-five per cent of the population of Saskatchewan and Alberta was rural, while the majority of Ontario's population was urban. Thus the west was distinctive in many ways.

When Alberta and Saskatchewan were created as provinces, they did not include the area in the far north. This area was made up of two separate territories, the Yukon and the North-West Territories. The Yukon, because of its prosperity during the Gold Rush, was made a separate district in 1898. The territories were governed by federally appointed commissioners and elected assemblies or councils.

ACTIVITIES

Check Your Understanding

1. Add these new words to your *Factfile*.

   • township • section • quarter section • Dominion Land Act • sod house
   • sodding bee • selected immigration • Red Fife • Marquis wheat • Trail of '98
   • panning for gold • rocker box • sluice box

2. Describe how the land in the West was made ready for settlers.

3. Why did people leave their homelands for Canada in the 1880s? Why do people move to Canada from other countries today?

4. What qualities did people need to be successful homesteaders on the prairies?

5. Explain why Clifford Sifton's advertising campaign was largely successful.

6. Read the poem by Robert Service, "The Spell of the Yukon" and list some of the reasons that could motivate people to go looking for gold.

7. What sorts of provisions were prospectors recommended to take with them to the goldfields? What does the list on page 162 tell you about their diets?

Confirm Your Learning

8. You have applied for a homestead in the prairie township shown on page 166. You are about to select the quarter section you want for your farm. The map on page 166 provides some information to help you make a decision.
   a) Number the sections in the township. Cross out the sections that are not available for homesteads.
   b) Examine the map and note the features of the land.
   c) List the advantages and disadvantages of each of these features from the point of view of a homesteader.
   d) Make a decision about which quarter section you would select as your homestead. Remember that you may wish to add adjoining land in the future. Give reasons for your choice.

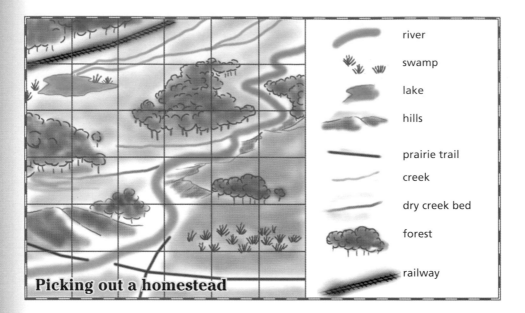

river

swamp

lake

hills

prairie trail

creek

dry creek bed

forest

railway

Picking out a homestead

9. Examine a road map of Manitoba, Saskatchewan, or Alberta. Look carefully at the names of the towns and villages. Do the names give you any clues about the nationalities of the people who settled there? For example, the people around Stockholm, Saskatchewan, were Swedish.

10. Imagine you are government agents attempting to encourage settlement in the Canadian West. Divide into three groups—the first to work in Britain, the second in Europe, and the third in the United States. Develop an advertising campaign, including posters, newspaper advertisements, etc., to attract settlers from your area of the world. If you have knowledge of other languages, use them on your poster.

11. Explain how the building of railways in western Canada affected:
    a) settlement
    b) growth of villages and towns
    c) growth of cities
    d) trade and export.

12. Collect pictures, draw diagrams, or construct models for a scrapbook or bulletin board display on life in the gold mines of the Klondike. Include captions, short stories, diary entries, newspaper reports, statistics, or charts.

13. Use the data in Table 1 on page 157 to create a bar graph to show the total number of immigrants who arrived in Canada from 1897 to 1905.

Challenge Your Mind

14. Divide your class into three groups. Imagine that you are about to move to a place that is quite different from where you are living now. One group is moving to a town in another region of Canada, one group is moving to a city in Australia, and one group is moving to a city in Saudi Arabia.

In your groups, discuss how this move will affect your way of life. What changes do you think will be easy to make? What changes will be difficult? What could you do to make these changes easier? What features of your present way of life would you not want to change?

List the changes and classify them under the headings of language, customs, technology, clothing, and values and beliefs. Elect a spokesperson from your group to present your ideas to the class.

15. Debate: Immigration is good for Canada.

16. Find out about other important Canadian inventors from the turn of the twentieth century. Examples include: Elijah McCoy, Reginald Fessenden, Sandford Fleming, Alexander Graham Bell, and Guglielmo Marconi.

17. Debate: The Northwest and Yukon territories should be granted provincial status.

Photo Credits

t = top
c = centre
b = bottom
BC Archives = British Columbia Archives and Records Management Services
Glenbow = Glenbow Archives, Calgary, Alberta
HBCA = Hudson's Bay Company Archives/Provincial Archives of Manitoba
MTRL = Metropolitan Toronto Reference Library
NAC = National Archives of Canada

1: NAC/C-4784; 2: MTRL/1086; 3: MTRL; 4: NAC/C-11095; 7: (t) The Law Society of Upper Canada Archives Photograph Collection/P1053, (b) Art Gallery of Ontario, Toronto/ Gift of the Cayley Sisters, Great-Granddaughters of Lady Robinson, 1953; 8: NAC/C-11818; 9: NAC/C-7043; 12: NAC/C-11095; 13: MTRL 1751; 14: NAC/C-70707; 16: (t) NAC/C-4785, (b) Karen Clark; 17: *A View of the Château-Richer, Cape Torment, and Lower End of the Isle of Orleans near Quebec* by Thomas Davies/National Gallery of Canada, Ottawa; 18: MTRL; 19: (t) NAC/C-18294, (c) NAC/C-393, (b) NAC/C-396; 21: (t) NAC/C-13392, (b) NAC/C-5456; 22: Tom Moore Photography, Toronto/Government of Ontario Art Collection, Toronto; 23: NAC/C-315; 26: MTRL 1964; 29: (t) Greenpeace/Gleizes, (b) Greenpeace/Vinai; 34: NAC; 36: NAC/PA-103906; 37: NAC/C-18737; 38: NAC/Bengough; 39: Courtesy of the Royal Ontario Museum, Toronto/71.1.117; 40: NAC/C-6512; 41: NAC; 43: NAC/C-733; 44: Courtesy Confederation Life; 45: NAC/PA-12632; 46: NAC/PA-25465; 51: Courtesy Confederation Life; 52: NAC/C-5812; 55: BC Archives/B6791; 56: (t) Malak Photographs, (b) Warren Toda/The Toronto Sun; 57: Ryan Remiore/Canapress; 60: HBCA; 62: (t) Comstock/Henry Georgi, (b) Comstock/Robert Hall; 63: (t) Darwin Wiggett/First Light, (b) Comstock/George Hunter; 64: Courtesy of the ROM; 66: (t) *Indian House Interior with Totems* by Emily Carr/Vancouver Art Gallery/Trevor Mills, (c) Glenbow Archives/NA-1431-28; (b) Courtesy of the Royal Ontario Museum, Toronto/Ethnology/955.177.28A-B; 68: BC Archives/C-9278; 69: (t) Courtesy of Head-Smashed-In-Buffalo-Jump/Alberta Culture and Multiculturalism, (b) Thomas Kitchin/First Light; 70: Pat Morrow/First Light; 71: Royal British Columbia Museum, Victoria, British Columbia/PN 242; 72: (t) Glenbow/ND-24-44, (c) BC Archives/F-8990, (b) BC Archives/I-23143; 76: Provincial Archives of Manitoba/N8722; 77: NAC/C-2774; 79: (t) Provincial Archives of Manitoba/N3937, (b) City of Lethbridge Archives and Records Management/ P19731723018; 81: Western Canada Pictorial Index; 83: (t) NAC/C-17726, (b) BC Archives/B06670; 84: NAC/C-73712; 85: Courtesy of the Native Sons of British Columbia and Simon Fraser University; 86: MTRL; 87: NAC/C-1572; 90: BC Archives/A-03081; 91: *Leather Pass* by William Hind/McCord Museum; 92: BC Archives/PDP02612; 93: BC Archives/A-06955; 94: BC Archives/A-3872; 95: BC Archives/A-00347; 98: BC Archives/G-5497; 102: HBCA/P-394; 103: HBCA/P-449; 104: (t) *Half Breeds Running Buffalo* by Paul Kane/Royal Ontario Museum, Toronto, (b) NAC/C-11021; 105: Saskatchewan Archives Board/R-A2294; 106: HBCA/P-393; 107: Provincial Archives of Manitoba/N5955; 109: NAC/C-6692; 110: BC Archives/PDP00501; 111: Prince Edward Island Archives and Records Office; 113: Glenbow/NA-1315-4; 114: NAC/C-95470; 116: NAC/C-8549; 117: (t) Glenbow/NA-1654-1, (b) NAC/PA-66576; 118: Provincial Archives of Alberta/E. Brown Collection/B-6022; 119: City of Vancouver Archives/ Can.P78.N52; 123: Courtesy of the Family of Yip Sai Gai; 125: NAC/C-069921; 126: Glenbow/NA-13-1; 127: The Granger Collection, New York; 128: NAC/C-56472; 129: NAC/PA-124101; 132: NAC/C-86515; 133: NAC/C-33058; 134: NAC/C-2424; 137: NAC/C-2769; 138: NAC/PA-28853; 139: (t) Glenbow/NA-1063-1, (c) NAC/PA-12197, (b) NAC/C-17430; 140: NAC/C-2769; 141: NAC/C-1879; 146: Glenbow/NA-1104-1; 147: Glenbow/NA-263-1; 148: Glenbow/NA-266-1; 150: Glenbow/NA-474-4; 151: (t) Peterborough Centennial Museum Archives, (c) Courtesy Canada Post, (b) Imperial Oil Ltd; 152: Western Canada Pictorial Index; 153: (t) Provincial Archives of Manitoba/ N9905, (b) Western Canada Pictorial Index; 154: NAC/C-85854; 155: (t) NAC/C-52819, (b) NAC/C-38706; 156: Glenbow/NA-984-2; 158: Saskatchewan Archives Board/R-A2435; 159: Provincial Archives of Manitoba/N7934; 161: NAC/PA-13482; 162: Courtesy Confederation Life; 163: Provincial Archives of Alberta/B.5280; 164: Glenbow/NA-1043-1.

Index

Note: Page numbers in boldface contain definitions of terms. Page numbers in *italics* indicate pictures. Code letters after page numbers indicate special kinds of material: *b* indicates boxed information; *c* indicates a caption; *f* indicates a figure; *m* indicates a map; and *t* indicates a table.